AmericanHeritage®

AMERICAN VOICES

WESTWARD EXPANSION

AmericanHeritage®
AMERICAN VOICES

WESTWARD EXPANSION

David C. King

WILEY

John Wiley & Sons, Inc.

Published by John Wiley & Sons, Inc., Hoboken, New Jersey
Published simultaneously in Canada

Design and production by Navta Associates, Inc.

American Heritage is a registered trademark of American Heritage Inc. Its use is pursuant to a license agreement.

For general information about our other products and services, please contact our Customer Care Department within the United States at (800) 762-2974, outside the United States at (317) 572-3993 or fax (317) 572-4002.

Wiley also publishes its books in a variety of electronic formats. Some content that appears in print may not be available in electronic books. For more information about Wiley products, visit our web site at www.wiley.com.

Library of Congress Cataloging-in-Publication Data

King, David C.
   Westward expansion / David C. King.
      p. cm. — (American Heritage, American voices)
   Summary: Uses letters, excerpts from journals and diaries, newspaper articles, and other primary source material to provide a look at life during the second half of the nineteenth century when many Americans moved westward.
   Includes bibliographical references (p.) and index.
   ISBN 0-471-44394-8 (acid-free paper)
      1. West (U.S.)—History—Sources—Juvenile literature. 2. West (U.S.)—Discovery and exploration—Sources—Juvenile literature. 3. West (U.S.)—Descripton and travel—Sources—Juvenile literature. 4. Frontier and pioneer life—West (U.S.)—Sources—Juvenile literature. 5. Pioneers—West (U.S.)—Biography—Juvenile literature. 6. United States—Territorial expansion—Sources—Juvenile literature. [1. West (U.S.)—History—Sources. 2. Frontier and pioneer life—West (U.S.)—Sources. 3. United States—Territorial expansion—Sources.] I. Title
F591.K49   2003
978'.02—dc21
                                                                        2003043277

Printed in the United States of America

10 9 8 7 6 5 4 3 2 1

CONTENTS

Introduction to the **AmericanHeritage**®
American Voices Series

For more than four hundred years of our nation's history, Americans have left a long paper trail of diaries, letters, journals, and other personal writings. Throughout this amazingly vast collection, we can often find intriguing information about the events that make up that history. A diary entry, for example, can help us feel we are on the scene, as in this army officer's entry on the eve of a critical Revolutionary War battle: "It is fearfully cold, and a storm setting in. The wind is northeast and beats in the faces of the men. It will be a terrible night for the soldiers who have no shoes."

These firsthand accounts can also present us with surprises. In 1836, for instance, Narcissa Whitman was warned that hardship and possibly death awaited her on the rugged Oregon Trail. But from the trail she wrote: "Our manner of living is preferable to any in the States [the East]. I never was so happy and content before. Neither have I enjoyed such health." And personal writings can also take us inside the minds of people caught up in events, as in the case of Clara Barton, who became famous as a battlefield nurse in the Civil War but first had to wrestle with doubts about whether it was proper for a woman to tend wounded soldiers. "I struggled long and hard," she wrote, "with the appalling fact that I was only a woman . . . [but] thundering in my ear were the groans of suffering men dying like dogs [to save the society] that had protected and educated me."

Intriguing fragments like these make up our nation's history. Journals, letters, diaries, and other firsthand accounts are called primary sources. In addition to letters and journals, other voices from the past emerge from newspapers, books, and magazines, from poems and songs, from advertisements, pamphlets, and government documents. Added to the written records are "visual documents" such as sketches, diagrams, patent designs, maps, paintings, engravings, and photographs.

Historians have the fascinating work of sifting through these fragments, searching for the ones that will add a special touch to their reconstruction of the past. But historians are not the only ones who can appreciate these details. America's huge storehouse of primary materials offers a great opportunity to make history more interesting, exciting, and meaningful to everyone. History textbooks are useful for providing the bare bones of history, but firsthand accounts add the muscle and sinew, fleshing out the story with the experiences of real men and women. Primary sources also let you come to your own conclusions about what happened in the past, and they help you make connections between the past and the present.

In creating this series, we've looked for selections that draw out the drama, excitement, tragedy, and humor that have characterized the American experience. The cast of characters comes from a variety of backgrounds and time periods, but they all have authentic American voices, and they have all contributed to our nation's story. We have kept most of the selections short in order to include as many different voices and viewpoints as possible.

The language of primary sources can be difficult. For this series, we have modernized some of the spelling and grammar so that the texts are easier to understand, while being careful to maintain the meaning and tone of the original. We have also provided vocabulary and background information in the margins to help you understand the texts. For the most part, however, we have let the American voices speak for themselves. We hope that what they have to say will interest you, sometimes surprise you, and even inspire you to learn more about America's history.

Introduction to *Westward Expansion*

On November 7, 1805, William Clark noted a special moment in his journal of the Lewis and Clark expedition: "Great joy in camp!" he wrote. "We are in view of the *Ocean*—this Great Pacific Ocean which we have been so long anxious to see."

To Americans in 1805, it was astounding that these men had actually crossed the continent. However, the idea that anyone could settle in that wilderness was almost impossible to imagine. And yet, through the 1800s, that's exactly what the pioneers did—risking their lives to go west and, in the process, launching one of the most remarkable migrations in history.

One of the most surprising things about America's westward movement was how quickly it happened. By 1848, just a decade after Clark's death, fifteen new states had been carved out of the West. And by 1890 the great movement was essentially over; the Census Bureau reported that there was no longer any open space that could be called a frontier.

Throughout this extraordinary chapter of our history, several generations of Americans experienced pioneering as a way of life. For them, the frontier was always there: a Promised Land that beckoned to them from just beyond the next row of hills. The primary sources in this book will enable you to travel with them as they give in to the lure of rich new farmland, or gold in California and silver in Colorado, or building a railroad across the continent. You'll recognize pioneers from the East and from Europe, and even from China, and some who had escaped from slavery or had been freed as a result of the Civil War.

Many of the men and women who lived this great adventure were convinced that God had chosen them to subdue this continent, even though it meant dispossessing the Native American tribes, fighting them and anyone else who stood in their way, including the French, the British, and the Mexicans. By conquering the land, and settling it, they came to believe that nothing was impossible. One of their most important gifts to later generations was this frontier spirit and the urge to find new frontiers to cross.

In *Westward Expansion,* you'll encounter some of the men, women, and young people who lived during the most thrill-packed century of our history. A young cowboy will tell how, after stopping a cattle stampede, he fired his six-gun to see if anyone was nearby, promptly setting off a new stampede. You'll study some of the pictures created by pioneer artists, paintings and engravings that enabled people in the East to visualize life on the frontier. You'll read the accounts of a number of pioneers describing their hardships and triumphs on the wagon trails to the West, and you will hear Chief Joseph of the Sioux explain why he would no longer fight.

One of the great advantages of working with primary sources is that they present the human side of history. After you've read Narcissa Whitman's account of the first wagon train on the Oregon Trail, or a "sodbuster's" description of battling a horde of grasshoppers, you'll understand the full meaning of the statement "People, not events, make history."

PART I

CROSSING THE FIRST MOUNTAIN BARRIER

When the American Revolution (1775–1783) transformed thirteen British colonies into the United States of America, most of the nation's three million people lived near the Atlantic coast. The land to the west was a vast, unknown wilderness of dark forests, forebidding mountains, and warlike Indian tribes. But a few daring pioneers had already begun pushing into that wild land. As early as the 1760s, some had crossed the first major barrier—the Appalachian Mountains, which stretched from Vermont in the North to Georgia in the South.

These first pioneers had no roads or trails to follow, and no maps to guide them. Once through the mountains, they found a paradise of fertile lands and magnificent rivers and streams, but they also encountered the many Native American tribes who claimed the same lands as their hunting grounds. The pioneer settlers were willing to buy the land when they could, or fight for it if they had to.

The readings in part I will give you some ideas about what these early pioneers faced.

Daniel Boone and the Appalachian Barrier

Map of the United States and its western territory, drawn in 1783—the year Americans won their independence from Great Britain.

Daniel Boone was one of the first pioneers determined to open the West. From his North Carolina farm, Boone began exploring through the Blue Ridge Mountains, part of the Appalachian chain, into the land called Kentucky west of the mountains. In 1775, after several years of this probing, he was hired by the Transylvania Company as an agent to buy land from the Native Americans. Boone organized a team of thirty woodsmen

6666666

to carve a trail from Virginia into Kentucky that became known as the "Wilderness Road."

Boone became well known for his trailblazing, but he became a legendary figure following the publication of his story in 1784. Although the book, which detailed his adventures on the frontier, was called an autobiography, it was really written by John Filson, a **land speculator,** who hoped it would draw settlers to Kentucky. The book was a great success and helped convince many families to follow Boone's Wilderness Road. By 1792, Kentucky had the 60,000 people needed to enter the Union as a new state, and Tennessee followed just four years later.

In the following selection, Boone describes some of his first impressions of the lands he explored in 1769 and 1770, and his first encounters with Shawnee warriors. The Shawnee and other tribes put up a fierce resistance before yielding their lands to white settlers. The reading offers clues about why Boone became such a hero and why his account led others to head west.

The title page of John Filson's account of Daniel Boone, published in 1784.

FROM
The Adventures of Colonel Daniel Boone

1784

It was on the first of May in the year 1769, that I resigned my domestic happiness for a time, and left my family and peaceable habitation on the Yadkin river, in North Carolina, to wander through the wilderness of America, in quest of the country of Kentucky, in company with John Finley, John Stewart, Joseph Holden, James Monay, and William Cool.

We proceeded successfully; and after a long and fatiguing journey, through a mountainous wilderness, in a westward direction, on the seventh day of June following we found ourselves on Red river, where John Finley had formerly been trading with the Indians, and, from the top of an eminence, saw with pleasure the beautiful level of Kentucky.

land speculator: a real estate agent who buys land at a low price, hoping to sell later for a large profit.

Colonel Boone

Boone held the rank of colonel in the Virginia militia during the American Revolution. (The militia were the citizen soldiers of early America, with virtually every adult male serving in his community; the militia elected their officers.) Officers in the militia or in the army were allowed to use their rank as a title for life.

The "Dark and Bloody Ground"

The white settlers faced a bitter struggle to wrest the tribal lands from the Shawnee and other tribes. During the 1790s, for example, people began referring to Kentucky as the "Dark and Bloody Ground." One reason: of the 290 men who formed the first territorial government, only about a dozen were still alive a decade later.

drove: a herd.

canebrake: a thicket.

vexatious: troubling or disturbing.

We found everywhere abundance of wild beasts of all sorts, through this vast forest. The buffalo were more frequent than I have seen cattle in the settlements, browzing on the leaves of the cane, or cropping the herbage on those extensive plains, fearless, because ignorant, of the violence of man. Sometimes we saw hundreds in a **drove,** and the numbers about the salt springs were amazing. In this forest, the habitation of beasts of every kind natural to America, we practiced hunting with great success, until the 22d day of December following. . . .

In the decline of the day, near Kentucky river, as we ascended the brow of a small hill, a number of Indians rushed out of a thick **canebrake** upon us, and made us prisoners. The Indians plundered us of what we had, and kept us in confinement 7 days, treating us with common savage usage. During this time we [showed] no uneasiness or desire to escape, which made them less suspicious of us; but in the dead of the night, as we lay in a thick canebrake by a large fire, when sleep had locked up their senses, my situation not disposing me for rest, I touched my companion, and gently awoke him. We improved this favourable opportunity, and departed, leaving them to take their rest, and speedily directed our course towards our old camp, but found it plundered, and the company dispersed and gone home. . . .

About this time, my brother, Squire Boon, with another adventurer, who came to explore the country shortly after us, was wandering through the forest, determined to find me if possible, and accidentally found our camp. So much does friendship triumph over misfortune, that sorrows and sufferings vanish at the meeting not only of real friends, but of the most distant acquaintances. . . .

One day I undertook a tour through the country, and the diversity and beauties of nature I met with in this charming season, expelled every gloomy and **vexatious** thought.

. . . I was surrounded with plenty in the midst of want. I

was happy in the midst of dangers and inconveniences. In such a diversity it was impossible I should be disposed to melancholy. No populous city, with all the varieties of commerce and stately structures, could afford so much pleasure to my mind, as the beauties of nature I found here.

. . . Soon after, I returned home to my family, with a determination to bring them as soon as possible to live in Kentucky, which I esteemed a second paradise, at the risk of my life and fortune.

The Kidnapping of Jemima Boone

The Shawnee and other tribes used various methods in their attempts to drive out the white settlers swarming into their lands. They tried to destroy new settlements, launching a dozen attacks on Boonesboro, the fortified village established by Boone in 1775. They also tried to terrorize the pioneers to convince them to turn back.

In July 1776, Boone's fourteen-year-old daughter Jemima and two friends were kidnapped by Shawnee warriors. Boone gave chase and followed the band for three days. The girls had the presence of mind to leave a trail by breaking twigs whenever possible and by tearing off tiny bits of clothing. Somehow, Boone managed to rescue the three without killing any of the warriors. Boone himself was captured by the Shawnee in February 1778, but managed to escape a few months later.

An artist's interpretation of Daniel Boone's rescue of his daughter Jemima. The painting was made in 1851, seventy-five years after the event, and the artist used more imagination than historical fact.

Opening the Northwest to Settlers

After America won independence from Great Britain in 1783, the U.S. Congress established two important laws for settling lands beyond the Appalachian Mountains. First, the Land Ordinance of 1785 established a national land-survey system for dividing new lands into townships and "sections." The Northwest Ordinance of 1787 provided for the new lands to be organized into territories when the population reached 60,000 and then to apply for admission to the Union as states. These laws guaranteed that settlers moving west would have their rights protected and that new states would enter the Union on an equal footing with the original thirteen states.

In the early 1800s, people began referring to this region as the "Old Northwest" to distinguish it from the Pacific Northwest (modern Oregon and Washington) acquired as part of the Louisiana Purchase in 1803. By the 1850s, as still more of the West was settled, the area from Ohio to Wisconsin became known as the Midwest.

The earliest settlements in the Old Northwest were organized in the late 1780s by the Ohio Company, formed by officers of the Revolutionary War, including George Washington. The company planned to organize settlements of at least 100 people. Colonel John May was one of the first settlers to establish the Ohio town of Marietta. The following selection describes some of the first days of the settlement.

FROM

Colonel John May's Journal

1788

Tuesday, May 27, 1788

. . . Have spent the day in reconnoitering the spot where the city is to be laid out, and find it to answer the best descriptions I have heard of it. The situation is delightfully agreeable, and well calculated for an elegant city. . . .

Thursday, 29th. This day the axe is laid to the root of the trees. . . . I was engaged in the afternoon with the surveyors. Find the soil very good, but was tormented beyond measure by myriads of gnats. They not only bit surprisingly, but get down one's throat. . . .

Sunday, 15th. A number of poor devils—five in all—took their departure homeward this morning. They came from home moneyless and brainless, and have returned as they came.

Tuesday, 17th. This evening Judge Parsons' and General Varnum's **commissions** were read; also, regulations for the government of the people. In fact, by-laws were much wanted. Officers were named to command the militia; guards to be mounted every evening; all males more than fifteen years old to appear under arms every Sunday.

Friday, [July] 4th. All labor comes to a pause to-day in memory of the Declaration of Independence. Our long **bowery** is built on the east bank of the Muskingum; a table laid sixty feet long, in plain sight of the garrison, one-quarter of a mile distant. At 1 o'clock General Harmer and his lady, Mrs. McCurders, and all the officers not on duty came over, and several other gentlemen. An excellent oration was delivered by Judge Varnum, and the cannon fired a salute of fourteen guns.

Wednesday, 9th. This is, in a sense, the birthday of this Western World. Governor St. Clair arrived at the garrison. His landing was announced by the discharge of fourteen cannon; and all rejoiced at his coming.

Obstacles to the Pioneers

Largely because of the organized settlements started by the Ohio Company, Ohio was soon ready for territorial status and was admitted as a state in 1803. However, the rest of the Old Northwest was settled more slowly. Much of the region was covered with dense forests. The pioneers faced disheartening labor just to clear enough land to plant their first crops.

The hostility of the Indian tribes was an even greater obstacle; periodic warfare and raids continued until 1830. During the forty-five years after Ohio statehood, only four more states were created in the Old Northwest—Indiana, Illinois, Iowa, and Wisconsin.

commissions: orders.
bowery: a shaded arbor.

PART II

JEFFERSON AND THE WEST

President Thomas Jefferson had been intrigued by the unknown, unexplored wilderness that stretched across the western half of the continent. His interest was increased by the historic voyages of a Boston trading vessel, the *Columbia*. The ship returned with news of the discovery of a great river that flowed into the Pacific. Jefferson was immediately filled with curiosity—did this river, named the Columbia, connect with the Missouri River somewhere in the Rocky Mountains? Such a connection would create a waterway through North America—a Northwest Passage that people had dreamed of and searched for for three hundred years.

In 1803, Jefferson persuaded Congress to fund an expedition to explore from the Mississippi River northwest on the Missouri toward the Pacific. Even before the Lewis and Clark expedition was fully organized, Jefferson and the Congress were able to purchase the Louisiana Territory from France. The territory covered 800,000 square miles west of the Mississippi River, including the region the expedition was to explore.

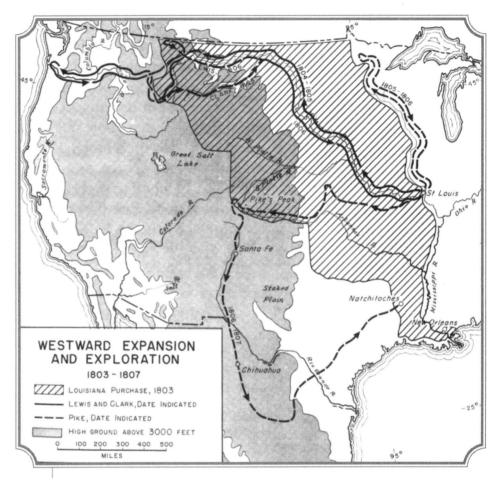

Westward expansion, 1803–1807, showing the route of the Lewis and Clark expedition and of army explorer Zebulon Pike, 1806–1807.

WESTWARD EXPANSION AND EXPLORATION
1803 – 1807

///// LOUISIANA PURCHASE, 1803
——— LEWIS AND CLARK, DATE INDICATED
- - - PIKE, DATE INDICATED
     HIGH GROUND ABOVE 3000 FEET
0   100   200   300   400   500
MILES

The Voyage of the *Columbia*

Between 1787 and 1793, sea captain Robert Gray made two historic voyages as commander of the trading vessel *Columbia*. After years of relying on trade with Great Britain and the British West Indies, America needed new markets, and the ship owners sent Gray on a new trading venture. From Boston, the *Columbia* first sailed around South America to what is now the Pacific Northwest (Oregon and Washington), a distance of 17,000 miles. The Americans traded with the Northwest tribes, exchanging such items as tools, nails, and trinkets for beaver and otter furs.

With a full hold, Captain Gray then sailed the *Columbia* to China, trading the furs for Chinese goods, such as tea, silk, porcelain, and chinaware. The *Columbia* continued westward, returning to Boston in 1790, and becoming the first American ship to sail around the world.

Gray's second voyage (1790–1793) was even more remarkable. While sailing along the Northwest coast, Gray and his crew spotted a magnificent river, which Gray named the Columbia. This was the river that led Thomas Jefferson to wonder about a Northwest Passage through the continent. In addition, the two voyages launched America's valuable new trade with China.

OREGON HISTORICAL SOCIETY

The ship Columbia, *painted by George Davidson, who was on the historic voyage.*

FROM

The Diary of John Boit

1792

May 17, 1792

This day saw an appearance of a spacious harbour abrest the Ship, haul'd our wind for itt, [*sic*] observ'd two sand bars making off, with a passage between them to a fine river. Out **pinnace** and sent her in ahead and followed with the Ship under short sail.

The [Columbia] River extended to the NE as far as eye cou'd reach, and water fit to drink as far down as the **Bars** at the entrance.

pinnace: a small sailing ship, used with larger vessels for short side trips or going ashore.

bars: sandbars that form near the mouth of a river.

We directed our course up this noble river in search of a Village. The beach was lin'd with Natives, who ran along shore following the Ship. Soon after above 20 Canoes came off, and brought a good lot of Furs and Salmon, which last they sold two for a board Nail; the furs were likewise bought cheap, for Copper and Cloth.

At length we arriv'd opposite to a large village, situate on the North side of the river about 5 **leagues** from the entrance, **came too** in 10 **fathom** sand about ¼ mile from shore.

The river at this place was about 4 miles over. We purchas'd 4 Otter Skins for a Sheet of Copper, Beaver Skins, 2 **Spikes** each and other land furs, 1 Spike each.

May 18
Capt. Gray named this river Columbia's. This River in my opinion wou'd be a fine place for to sett up a Factory; the river abounds with excellent Salmon.

May 20
We lay in this place till the 20th May, during which time we put the Ship in good order and fill'd up the water casks along side, itt being very good. The Indians inform'd us there was 50 Villages on the banks of this river. . . .

league: a unit of measure equal to three miles.

came to: stopped, or lowered an anchor.

fathom: a nautical unit of measure equal to six feet.

spikes: large nails.

Chinese Imports

From the 1790s on, products from China were a rage in America. Even families without great wealth could enjoy the tea and spices, or buy "chinaware"—pottery that was so inexpensive it was used in the holds of ships for ballast (weight to help balance the cargo). In addition, a soft Chinese cotton called nankeen became the favorite fabric for men's clothing and led to a fashion change from knee-length breeches to more modern-looking trousers. The homes of wealthier Americans displayed Chinese items of great beauty, such as silk wall hangings or screens, delicate carvings in jade or ivory, and porcelain vases or figurines.

The Lewis and Clark Expedition

President Jefferson appointed his personal secretary, Meriwether Lewis, to lead the expedition along with William Clark, younger brother of George Rogers Clark, a hero of frontier warfare in the American Revolution. In May 1804 the "Corps of Discovery" set off from St. Louis with forty-five men, nearly all volunteers from the army. Jefferson charged Lewis and Clark with finding out all they could about the land, the people, and the plant and animal life in the territory. In addition, he wanted them to find out if the Missouri River connected with the Columbia to form a waterway to the Pacific.

For much of the journey, a French-Canadian trader named Touissant Charboneau served as a guide. Charboneau's young wife, Sacagawea (or Sacajawea), proved to be a most valuable addition. A member of the Shoshone or Snake tribe, Sacagawea had been captured by a tribe called the Hidatsa as a child and sold as a slave. Charboneau rescued her and she seems to have eagerly accompanied her husband and the "Long Knives," as she called the explorers, on their journey.

Several of the men with Lewis and Clark wrote about the historic expedition, and there were also different versions of the journals kept by the two leaders. The first portion of the journals used here was written by Nicholas Biddle, using manuscripts and notes given to him by Captain Clark; the second was written by Lewis himself. The first reading provides

The Lewis and Clark expedition as depicted in a twentieth-century mural. Sacagawea and her husband are on the right, between the two canoes.

OREGON HISTORICAL SOCIETY

Completing the Journey

When the expedition reached the Pacific Coast, they hoped to sail home on a New England ship that was supposed to be there to trade with the natives of the coast. When no ship appeared, they decided to return overland. For several months there was no word of their whereabouts, and most Americans assumed they had been overwhelmed by Indians. When they suddenly appeared in St. Louis in September 1806, their arrival touched off a nationwide celebration. Through twenty-eight months of hardship and difficulties, they had traveled more than 8,000 miles. They had encountered fifty tribes without any major conflicts. Only one man was lost, probably from a ruptured appendix.

a glimpse of Sacagawea and of Shoshone life; the second selection, describing an encounter with a grizzly bear, indicates the kind of dangers the explorers faced every day.

ℐℐ ℐℐ ℐℐ ℐℐ ℐℐ ℐℐ ℐℐ ℐℐ ℐℐ ℐℐ ℐℐ ℐℐ ℐℐ ℐℐ ℐℐ

FROM

The Journals of Lewis and Clark

1805

On setting out at seven o'clock, Captain Clarke with Charboneau and his wife walked on shore, but they had gone not more than a mile before Clarke saw Sacajawea, who was with her husband 100 yards ahead, began to dance and show every mark of the most extravagant joy, turning round him and pointing to several Indians, whom he saw advancing on horseback, sucking her fingers at the same time to indicate that they were of her native tribe.

We soon drew near to the camp, and just as we approached it a woman made her way through the croud [*sic*] towards Sacajawea, and recognising each other, they embraced with the most tender affection. The meeting of these two young women had in it something pecularly touching.

While Sacajawea was renewing among the women the friendships of former days, Captain Clarke went on, and was received by Captain Lewis and the chief, who after the first embraces and salutations were over, conducted him to a sort of circular tent or shade of willows.

Here he was seated on a white robe; and the chief immediately tied in his hair six small shells resembling pearls, an ornament highly valued by these people, who procure them in the course of trade from the seacoast. The moccasins of the whole party were then taken off, and after much ceremony the smoking began.

After this the conference was to be opened, and glad of an opportunity to be able to converse more intelligibly, Sacajawea was sent for; she came into the tent, sat down, and was beginning to interpret, when she recognized her brother; She instantly jumped up, and ran and embraced him; throwing over him her blanket and weeping profusely; The chief was himself moved, though not in the same degree.

After some conversation between them she resumed her seat, and attempted to interpret for us, but her new situation seemed to overpower her, and she was frequently interrupted by her tears. After the council was finished the unfortunate woman learnt that all her family were dead except two brothers, one of whom was absent, and a son of her eldest sister, a small boy, who was immediately adopted by her.

The End of Northwest Passage Dreams

When the explorers reached the headwaters of the Missouri River, they thought they were only about ten miles from the Columbia River. They were wrong. The distance was much greater and the terrain was so difficult it took them nine weeks to reach the Columbia—harsh facts that ended the dream of finding a Northwest Passage.

FROM

The Journal of Meriwether Lewis

1805

In the evening, the men in two of the rear canoes discovered a large brown bear. He was lying on the open ground. Six of them went out to attack him. They were all good hunters. They got within forty paces of him without being seen.

Two of them saved their fire as had been planned. The four others fired nearly at the same time and each put his bullet through him. Two of the balls passed through his lungs.

In an instant, this monster ran at them with open mouth. The two who had saved their fires now fired. Both of them struck him, one only slightly. The other fortunately broke his shoulder, but this only slowed his motion for a moment.

The men, unable to reload their guns, took to flight. The bear pursued and had very nearly overtaken them before they reached the river. Two of the party went to a canoe. The others separated and hid among the willows.

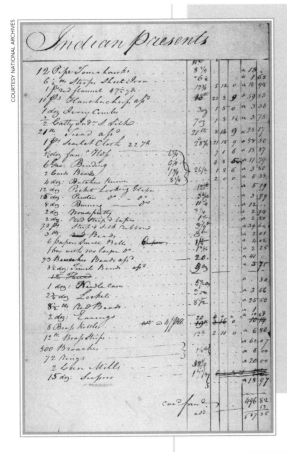

A list of gifts Meriwether Lewis purchased to give to tribal leaders the expedition encountered, including things like twelve pipe tomahawks and one dozen ivory combs.

They reloaded their pieces. Each fired at him as they had an opportunity. They struck him several times, but the guns served only to direct the bear to them. In this manner, he pursued two of them separately. He was so close that they had to throw away their guns and dive into the river.

So enraged was this animal that he plunged into the river only a few feet behind the second man. One of those who still remained on shore shot him through the head and finally killed him.

They then took him on shore and butchered him. They found that eight balls had passed through him in different directions. The bear being old, the flesh was not very good. They therefore took only the skin and fleece [the coat]. The latter made us several gallons of oil.

The Explorations of Zebulon Pike

In 1806, the governor of Louisiana Territory named Zebulon Pike, an army officer, to lead an expedition into what is now the Southwest of the United States. Pike mapped a route southwest from St. Louis but was stopped by Spanish soldiers in New Mexico, a Spanish province. He was released in 1807, without his maps or notes, but he relied on memory to publish an account of his journey in 1810. This was the first account of the Southwest in English and added to the growing interest in the lands beyond the Mississippi.

Pike, who failed in an attempt to scale the mountain later named Pike's Peak, became a brigadier general in the War of 1812. He was killed while leading a successful attack on the Canadian town of York (present day Toronto).

PART III

Transportation in the Old Northwest

Transportation was a special problem for settlers heading west. Until nearly 1800, there was not a single wagon road west of the Appalachian Mountains. As late as 1837, roads were still so bad in places that a traveler reported that a stage coach ride from Pittsburgh to Erie, Pennsylvania, a distance of 128 miles, took 46 hours—a speed of less than 3 miles an hour.

One of the keys to settling the western frontier was improvement in transportation. The readings in this part will show what improvements were made and how they influenced the movement west.

Road Building: The National Road

In 1810 Congress approved funds for a great road that would stretch from Cumberland, Maryland, to Wheeling (in present-day West Virginia), about 250 miles. Work began in 1811, and by 1820 this National Road was crowded with pioneers heading west and freight wagons moving east, loaded with farm produce to sell in the cities and towns on the Atlantic seaboard. By 1830 the road reached Indiana. In the following selection, a traveler describes the National Road.

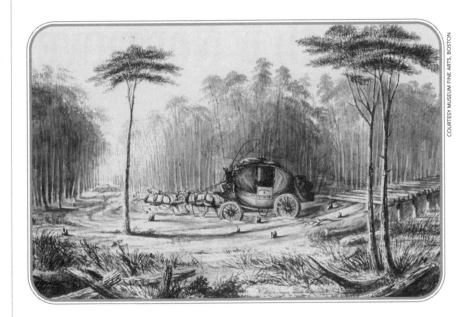

COURTESY MUSEUM FINE ARTS, BOSTON

George Tattersall's drawing of a stagecoach laboring over bad roads in the late 1820s.

FROM

Charles Latrobe's The Rambler in North America

C. 1825

The National Road, as they call it, is a permanent turnpike, built of stone, and covered with gravel. The central strip, about twenty feet wide, is crowned so that water is shed on either side, making this the only American road I have seen that is dry and passable in all seasons. . . . Throughout the eastern section, noble arches of stone have been thrown . . . over all the ravines and watercourses.

One is rarely out of sight of **emigrants** moving west. Many are families of four to seven members, all but one or two walking alongside a horse-drawn wagon that seems to hold all their wordly possessions. They set up camp in clearings along the way, a pleasant stopover at least in fair weather. Those who can afford to . . . [stop] at one of the inns where the fortunate ones will obtain a decent meal and a clean bed. . . .

A pleasant sight is provided by the great wagons called Conestogas. Drawn by four or six horses, and topped by a . . . sloping canvas roof, they look like sailing ships gliding majestically across the gravel sea.

emigrants: people moving from one place to another. By 1820, this was a common term to describe settlers heading west.

Travel on the Erie Canal

In 1816, the New York State legislature approved Governor De Witt Clinton's plan for a canal that would connect Lake Erie with the Hudson River at Albany. Ships could then travel all the way from the Great Lakes to the Atlantic Ocean at New York. The construction of "Clinton's Ditch" was a mammoth undertaking, especially in an age when all the work relied on hand tools, like shovels and pickaxes, not steam shovels or bulldozers.

When completed in 1825, the Erie Canal reduced travel time between Buffalo and New York City from more than twenty days to seven or eight; the cost of shipping grain east fell from $100 a ton to $15. For emigrants, travel on the canal offered a new kind of adventure—and some misadventures as well. From Buffalo, pioneers could take a Great Lakes steamboat to Detroit or take a flatboat or keelboat down the Ohio and then the Mississippi.

The next selection describes a journey on the canal in the early 1830s.

Frederick Gerstaecker's Journal

After breakfast I had plenty of time to notice the company with whom I shared the narrow space of a cabin in a canal boat. There were ten gentlemen and three ladies; these latter had a cabin to themselves, separated from the other by a red curtain; over the entrance was the inscription, "Ladies' Cabin," with the friendly reminder of "No Admittance." . . . These canal boats are very long and narrow, decked over, and rising about six feet above the water; ours was fitted up for the comfort, or rather discomfort of the passengers. They are well provided with windows, hold a number of people, and go very slowly; ours in particular, drawn by two very quiet horses, seemed to traverse the landscape at a snail's pace. The canal is crossed by numerous low bridges, often only a few inches above the deck, and one must be constantly on the look-out not to be swept overboard, a disaster I once happened to witness. Sometimes it is necessary to lie quite flat, a precaution which also has its dangers, and on one occasion caused a dreadful misfortune, when a passenger, by a boat that had very little cargo, was horribly crushed to death between the boat and the bridge. . . .

. . . The sleeping-places in the canal boats consist of long four-cornered frames which in the evening are hung up along the cabin; and now that the number of passengers had so much increased, we had to be packed in layers. The frames are covered with coarse strong canvas, on which a small mattress was laid . . . but now, on account of the number of new arrivals, that luxury had to be dispensed with. . . .

I awoke in the night with a dreadful feeling of suffocation; cold perspiration stood on my forehead, and I could hardly draw my breath; there was a weight like lead on my stomach and chest. I attempted to cry out—in vain; I lay almost without consciousness. At last I became quite awake, and remembered where I was. . . . The weight remained immovable; above me was a noise like distant thunder: it was my companion of the upper story, who lay snoring over my head. . . . I bethought me of my breastpin, which luckily I had not taken out of my cravat the night before; with great difficulty I succeeded in moving my arm and reaching the pin which I pressed with a firm hand into the mass above. "What's that?" "Murder!" "Help!" cried a deep bass voice above me. Feeling myself free, I slipped like an eel from under the weight, and saw, by the dim light reflected from a lamp hanging under the deck. . . . A stout heavy man, who slept in the upper frame without a mattress, was too much for the well-worn canvas, during his sleep it had given way under the weightiest part of his form, which descended till it found support on my chest.

The Erie Canal

The canal boats started from Albany at sea level. Over the 360 miles of the canal, they passed through 83 **locks** and climbed a total of 565 feet. Side canals connected to Lake Ontario at Oswego and to Lake Seneca. Swift boats, called packets, could cover the distance between Albany and Buffalo in six days by traveling night and day at a top speed of four miles per hour.

The canal crossed valleys on aqueducts—long wooden troughs built on stone piers. There were eighteen aqueducts.

lock: a section of a canal that can be closed off by gates in order to raise or lower the water level of the section.

The Erie Canal, painted by John William Hill, 1829.

Low Bridge, Everybody Down

There were dozens of Erie Canal songs, including the one printed here, written sometime in the 1820s, which was called "Low Bridge, Everybody Down," or "Fifteen Years on the Erie Canal," or "Song of the Mule Drivers."

I've got a mule, her name is Sal,
Fifteen miles on the Erie Canal.
She's a good old worker and a good old pal,
Fifteen miles on the Erie Canal.
We've haul'd some barges in our day,
Fill'd with lumber, coal and hay.
And we know ev'ry inch of the way
From Albany to Buffalo.

Refrain:

Low bridge, ev'rybody down!
Low bridge, for we're going through a town.
And you'll always know your neighbor,
You'll always know your pal,
If you ever navigated on the Erie Canal.

Houseboats, Flatboats, and Keelboats

In the early 1800s, a wide variety of crafts appeared on western waterways, especially the Ohio and Mississippi Rivers. Some vessels, with no sails or paddle wheels, were one-way boats that just traveled with the current. When the emigrants had gone as far as they could, they usually broke up the boat and sold the lumber, or used it to start their new home.

The keelboats were different because they could go upstream. Pointed at both ends, a keelboat could be poled upstream, with from five to fifteen men pushing poles to the shallow bottom. They could also be rowed or, on a long, straight stretch, a sail could be raised. Large keelboats could carry up to fifty tons of cargo. They were especially useful on the Missouri River, where westward-bound travelers were actually going against the river's west-to-east current.

The next two selections offer a glimpse of travel by flatboat and by keelboat in the late 1820s and early 1830s.

FROM

John Hall's Letters from the West

1827

To-day we passed two large rafts lashed together, by which simple conveyance several families from New England were transporting themselves and their property to the land of promise in the western woods. Each raft was eighty or ninety feet long, with a small house erected on it; and on each was a stack of hay, round which several horses and cows were feeding, while the paraphernalia of a farm-yard, the ploughs, waggons [*sic*], pigs, children, and poultry, carelessly distributed, gave to the whole more the appearance of a permanent residence, than of a caravan of adventurers seeking a home. A respectable looking old lady, with spectacles on nose, was seated on a chair at the door of one of the cabins, employed in knitting.

FROM

H. S. Tanner's Emigrant's and Traveller's Guide to the West

1834

The keel boats find much to do, during that portion of the summer and autumn when the river is too low for the steamboats to run. Hundreds of flat bottom boats . . .

When the Mississippi Flowed North!

Robert Fulton had established the first successful steamboat line on the Hudson River in New York. His hopes of repeating that success on the Mississippi River were thwarted when a devastating earthquake struck the Mississippi region. The upheaval of the bare rock was so severe that, for a short time, the huge river reversed direction and flowed north!

annually float down from a thousand places on the Ohio and other western streams, to Cincinnati or Louisville, or New Orleans. . . .

This mode of navigation is slow . . . but it is cheap. . . . Convenient and pleasant as is a steamboat . . . yet there are hundreds and thousands . . . who prefer the flat boat. . . .

These boats, however, are not only subject to great delays, but also exposed to some dangers from the rapids, sandbars, rocks, and sudden and violent storms and tornadoes, which can sink them. . . . Considering the form of these boats . . . it is truly wonderful that more accidents of this kind do not happen. . . .

There is not on earth a class of men of a more peculiar and marked character, than the western boatmen. . . . They have, it is true, lost much of the lawless and outrageous spirit which they had in the olden time, and before the introduction of steamboats upon the western waters . . . but their distinguishing traits of character remain—boldness, readiness to encounter almost any danger, recklessness of consequences, and indifference to the wants of the future, amid the enjoyments, the noise, whiskey and fun of the present.

Steamboats: Floating Palaces of the West

The first steamboat paddled down the Ohio and the Mississippi in 1811. By 1830, roughly 350 steamboats plied the western rivers. The boats were powered by steam engines that turned paddle wheels either on the side of the steamboat or in the stern; firewood heated water in the boiler to produce the steam. The quality and size of the boats varied widely. Most owners and captains were proud of their vessels and did everything they could for the comfort and pleasure of their passengers. They also hired river pilots to guide the boat through dangerous river passages where submerged rocks and other hazards could lead to a wreck. On smaller, cheaper steamboats the owner, captain, and pilot were usually the same person, which helped make every trip an uncertain adventure.

The selection below is from a minister named Timothy Flint. Flint traveled widely through frontier America in the 1820s and 1830s, distributing Bibles for a missionary society. His *Recollections of the Last Ten Years* was widely read.

FROM

Timothy Flint's Recollections of the Last Ten Years

1826

A stranger to this mode of travelling, would find it difficult to describe his impression upon first descending the Mississippi in one of the better steamboats. He contemplates the prodigious establishment, with all its fitting of deck, common, and ladies' cabin apartments. Over head, about him and below him, all is life and movement. He sees its splendid cabin, richly carpeted, its finishings of mahogany, its mirrors and fine furniture, its bar-room, and sliding tables, to which eighty passengers can sit down with comfort. The fare is sumptuous, and everything in a style of splendour, order, quiet, and regularity, far exceeding that of taverns in general. You read, you converse, you walk, you sleep, as you choose; for custom has prescribed that everything shall be **"sans ceremonie."** The varied and **verdant** scenery shifts around you.

. . . At other times you are sweeping along for many leagues . . . the cheerfulness of a floating hotel, which carries, perhaps, two hundred guests, contrasts with a wild and uninhabitable forest, one hundred miles in width, the abode only of owls, bears, and **noxious** animals,—this strong contrast produces to me at least, something of the same pleasant sensation that is produced by lying down to sleep with the rain pouring on the roof, immediately overhead.

sans ceremonie: a French term meaning simple, without ceremony (or fuss).

verdant: green, filled with plant life.

noxious: harmful or dangerous.

Steamboat Dangers

The great rivers of the West, including the Mississippi, Missouri, and the Ohio, challenged the steamboat's captain and the pilot. Tree trunks formed deadly "snags," and sandbars could appear overnight. Many of the boats were hastily built and the steam boilers sometimes overheated and exploded.

Perhaps the greatest danger arose when one steamboat started to pass another. The passengers on both boats would then take up the chant "Go ahead! Go ahead!"—urging their captain to tie down the safety valve, pour more wood on the boiler fire, and race. A race might be a great thrill, lasting hours, or it could be a disaster if one boat hit a snag or a boiler exploded.

A Currier and Ives lithograph of a famous 1870 steamboat race, the Robert E. Lee *beating the* Natchez.

LIBRARY OF CONGRESS

PART IV

DAILY LIFE IN THE OLD NORTHWEST

From the 1820s through the 1840s, pioneer families gradually filled in the lands around the southern rim of the Great Lakes and down the valley of the Mississippi River. Once the land had been cleared and farms built, people had time for other pursuits—starting schools, establishing businesses, and building towns. The way of life that emerged on the frontier was like eastern life in some ways, but there were also noticeable differences. As the readings in this section will indicate, frontier life still had some rough edges.

The Character of the Frontiersman

The first settlers in any region tended to be a rough lot. In many cases, they kept a loaded rifle close at hand day and night to fend off Indian war parties. Many people in the East thought of the frontier families as barely human—rough-living, hard-drinking men and women who were ready to move as soon as they could see smoke rising from a neighbor's cabin. In the following selection, Timothy Flint tries to present a more balanced view.

FROM

Timothy Flint's Recollections of the Last Ten Years

1 8 2 6

The people in the Atlantic states have not yet recovered from the horror inspired by the term "backwoodsman." When I first visited this country, I had my full share. I heard a thousand stories of **gougings** and robberies and shooting down with the rifle. I have travelled in these regions thousands of miles under all circumstances of exposure and danger. I never have carried the slightest weapon of defense. I scarcely remember to have experienced anything that resembled insult, or to have felt myself in danger from the people. . . .

The backwoodsman of the West, as I have seen him, is generally an amiable and virtuous man. His general motive for coming here is to be a **freeholder,** to have plenty of rich land, and to be able to settle his children about him. It is a most virtuous motive. I fully believe that nine in ten of the emigrants have come here with no other motive. You find, in truth, that he has vices and barbarisms peculiar to his situation. His manners are rough. He wears, it may be, a long beard. He has a great quantity of bear or deer skins wrought into his household establishment, his furniture, and dress. He carries a knife, or a dirk, in his bosom, and when in the

gougings: swindles, or crooked dealings.

freeholder: a landowner.

woods has a rifle on his back, and a pack of dogs at his heels. An Atlantic stranger, transferred directly from one of our cities to his door, would recoil from an encounter with him. But remember that his rifle and his dogs are among his chief means of support and profit. Remember that all his first days here were passed in dread of the savages. Enter his door, and tell him you are **benighted,** and wish the shelter of his cabin for the night. The welcome is indeed seemingly ungracious. But this apparent ungraciousness is the **harbinger** of every kindness that he can bestow, and every comfort that his cabin can afford. Good coffee, corn bread and butter, venison, pork, wild and tame fowls are set before you. You are shown to the best bed which the house can offer. When this kind of hospitality has been afforded you as long as you choose to stay, and when you depart, and speak about your bill, you are most commonly told with some slight mark of resentment that they do not keep a tavern.

benighted: overtaken by darkness while traveling.

harbinger: a sign of what is to come.

The First Schools in the Northwest

From Ohio in the East around the Great Lakes to Wisconsin in the West, every community built a schoolhouse soon after laying out a town. The buildings were rough, and so was the quality of the lessons—as described in the next selection by a man who grew up in frontier Michigan in the 1840s.

FROM

Edmund Barber's Recollections

C. 1840

The schoolhouse was a very primitive structure. The logs . . . were chinked on the inside with triangular pieces of basswood . . . fastened to the logs with nails . . . and were

McGuffey's Readers

William Holmes McGuffey (1800–1873) created *the* schoolbooks that were used in thousands of schools throughout the nation, but especially in the Old Northwest. The first *McGuffey's Reader* was published in 1836 and more than 120 million were sold by the end of the century. The *Readers* provided reading instruction along with stories, poems, interesting facts, and basic values like honesty and thrift. McGuffey was also a Presbyterian preacher and said that he had delivered 3,000 sermons without notes.

mudded on the outside to keep out the cold. . . . Around the room on three sides were wooden desks fastened to the logs and with a downward slant towards the long benches on which the scholars sat. . . . Not much mixing of the sexes was allowed. At the front, lighted by the east window, the teacher had a wooden chair, a plain **deal** table, on which was an inkstand and quill pen, a ruler, and the few books that constituted his equipment, and back of it on pegs driven into a log lay two or three whips from the woods, the insignia of his authority and power to punish for the infraction of the rules he had laid down to govern his pupils. . . .

The education . . . served a good purpose in after life, and seemed to be all that was essential to getting on in the world. . . . We learned to spell, read and write, with something of arithmetic, a little of geography, and a very little of grammar. The books used were of a motley character such as the first settlers brought with them from New England.

Frontier Medicine: A Cure for Rattlesnake Bite

There were few trained doctors in the Old Northwest, so people relied on an endless variety of home remedies. A common cure for rattlesnake bite involved cutting the snake into small pieces, splitting them open, and placing each piece, in turn, on the wound to draw out the poison. When this was done, the entire snake was burned as revenge for the damage it had caused. A compound of boiled chestnut leaves was then placed on the bite and this was repeated for several days. Sometimes the patient recovered.

deal: plain pine boards.

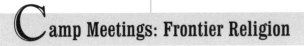

Camp Meetings: Frontier Religion

Religion has always been an important part of America's story. In addition to regular church services, periodic "revivals" have pumped new energy into many branches of Protestantism. Energetic ministers, or preachers, manage to electrify congregations, persuading many to confess their sins and dedicate themselves to God. Pioneer Americans flocked to these "camp meetings" with great enthusiasm, often becoming highly emotional or experiencing some kind of "fits." In the following selection, Peter Cartwright, one of the most famous revivalists, describes the camp meetings of the 1820s and 1830s.

FROM

Peter Cartwright's Autobiography

1 8 5 6

The people . . . came in their large wagons, with **victuals** mostly prepared. The women slept in the wagons, and the men under them. . . . The power of God was wonderfully displayed; scores of sinners fell under the preaching, like men slain in mighty battle. . . . They would erect a shed and . . . collect together from forty to fifty miles around. . . . Ten, twenty, and sometimes thirty ministers, of different denominations, would come together and preach night and day, four or five days together; and . . . I have known these camp meetings to last three or four weeks . . . and I have seen and heard more than five hundred Christians all shouting aloud the high praises of God at once.

victuals: food

COURTESY NEW YORK HISTORICAL SOCIETY

A frontier revival meeting.

Johnny Appleseed

Preachers and merchants who traveled the Old Northwest sometimes ran into a frontier character known as Johnny Appleseed. He wandered the region planting small groves of apple trees. So many legends grew around him that some doubted that he ever existed.

Johnny Appleseed was real. His given name was John Chapman. He was born in Massachusetts and moved to Pennsylvania about 1800. He collected apple seeds from cider mills, then headed into the western frontier. He seems to have wandered the countryside barefoot, wearing a simple linen robe—his "coat"—which served him in all seasons. He must have been a skilled nurseryman, and he either stayed near his plantings or returned often enough to be sure the trees were well started. There is no real evidence that any of his orchards still exist. Chapman was also a follower of a Swedish religious sect called Swedenborgism and spread the society's writings wherever he went.

Portrait of Jenny Lind, 1847; lithograph by Richard James Lane.

LIBRARY OF CONGRESS

Jenny Lind: The "Swedish Nightingale"

Frontier Americans were very fond of drama and of music. One of the most popular performers of the 1840s and early 1850s was Jenny Lind, billed as the "Swedish Nightingale." With her spellbinding voice and charming personality, she captivated audiences wherever she sang. Her tour manager was a young entrepreneur named Phineas T. Barnum, who was to gain even greater fame for his circus. Barnum introduced a new trend in marketing by having all sorts of Jenny Lind objects for sale wherever she performed. This was probably the first time that a performer's fame led to the creation of dolls, plates, jewelry, and countless other items.

The New Cities of the First West

Within twenty years of the first frontier settlements, some of the towns mushroomed into cities. Although many pioneers had headed west to find open space and new lands, once they were settled, large numbers became eager to build towns and cities that would rival the communities they had left behind in the East.

In the next selection, a traveler describes the changes he saw in Lexington, Kentucky, in the space of just nineteen years.

FROM

Samuel R. Brown's Report

1817

In the summer of 1797 [Lexington] contained about 50 houses, partly frame, and hewn logs; . . . the surrounding country was then new; a village lot could have been purchased for $30, and a good farm . . . for five dollars an acre. The best farmers lived in log cabins, and wore hunting shirts and leggings.

In May (1816) . . . how changed the scene! Everything had assumed a new appearance. . . . The log cabins had disappeared, and in their places stood costly brick mansions, well painted and enclosed by fine yards. . . . The leathern pantaloons, the hunting shirts and leggings had been discarded. . . . Main Street presents to the traveller as much wealth and more beauty than can be found in most of the Atlantic cities. It is about 80 feet wide . . . well paved and having **foot ways** on each side.

I was surprised to see at every step, finely painted brick stores, three stories high, and well filled with costly and fanciful merchandize [*sic*]. Near the center of town is the public square, lined on every side with large substantial houses,

foot ways: sidewalks.

elocution: the style and manner of public speaking.

rhetoric: skillful speaking.

stores, hotels, etc. . . . . This town appears as large and populous as Cincinnati, which contained in 1816, 1000 houses and 6000 souls. The public buildings consist of several churches. . . . There is a female academy, where the following branches are taught: reading, writing, arithmetic, grammar, correspondence, **elocution, rhetoric,** geography, astronomy, ancient and modern history, chronology, mythology, music, drawing, embroidery, etc. The taverns and boarding houses are neat and well furnished. . . . There are two bookstores, and three printing offices. . . . The inhabitants are as polished, as luxurious as those of Boston, New-York or Baltimore; and their assemblies are conducted with as much ease and grace, as in the oldest towns of the union.

PART V

NATIVE AMERICAN RESISTANCE AND THE INDIAN REMOVAL POLICY

From the time the American pioneers first crossed the Appalachian Mountains, they encountered bitter resistance from the Native American tribes. The British in Canada, anxious to keep the Americans from expanding their territory to the north, aided the Indians, creating one of the reasons the United States fought the British a second time in the War of 1812. Many tribes joined a force led by a Shawnee warrior named Tecumseh. When Tecumseh was killed in the War of 1812, Indian resistance faded in the Old Northwest.

In the 1830s, the government under President Andrew Jackson launched the Indian Removal Policy, forcing nearly all eastern tribes to move west of the Mississippi River to "Indian Territory." The U.S. Army "escorted" the tribes on what the Indians called the "Trail of tears." The president and Congress hoped that the removal of the Indians would end bloodshed but, even as the eastern Indians were entering Indian Territory, pioneers were crossing the Mississippi in ever-increasing numbers.

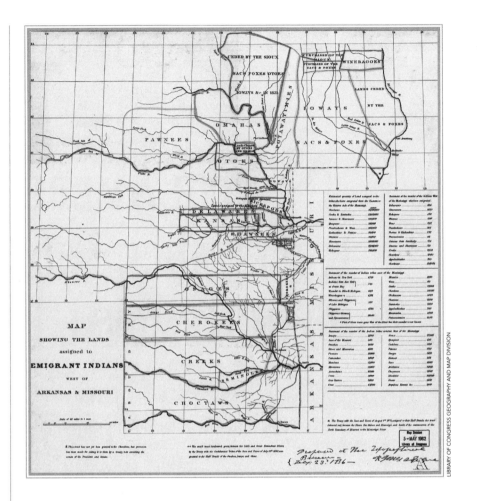

An 1836 map showing the lands assigned to the eastern tribes during the Indian Removal program. The lands west of the Missouri and Arkansas Rivers were designated as "Indian Territory." In the 1850s most of that land was opened to settlers.

Tecumseh: The Dream of Indian Unity

Tecumseh (1768–1813) was a Shawnee warrior who hoped to unite the tribes of the Northwest and Mississippi River Valley to create a force strong enough to drive the American settlers back toward the Atlantic coast. With his brother, a religious mystic the Americans called "the Prophet," they built a fortified settlement at Tippecanoe in Indian Territory.

While Tecumseh was away in November 1811, the Indian stronghold, called Prophetstown, was attacked and destroyed by a militia force led by William Henry Harrison, governor of Indian Territory. Two years later, in the War of 1812, Tecumseh was killed while fighting alongside the British. The dream of Indian unity died with him.

The following reading gives one of Tecumseh's speeches, as written down by a frontier soldier named General Sam Dale. Dale said of Tecumseh, "I have heard many great orators, but I never saw one with the vocal powers of Tecumseh, or with the same command of the muscles of his face. Had I been deaf, the play of his countenance would have told me what he said."

Tecumseh, the great Shawnee chief.

FROM

General Sam Dale's Report on Tecumseh

1811

Accursed be the race that has seized our country, and made women of our warriors! Our fathers, from their tombs, reproach us as slaves and cowards; I hear them now in the wailing winds.

The [Creeks] were once a mighty people. . . . Now your blood is white; your tomahawks have no edge; your bows and arrows were buried with your fathers. Oh, [Creeks] brush from your eyelids the sleep of slavery; once more strike for vengeance, once more for your country. The spirits of the mighty dead complain. The tears drop from the weeping sky. Let the white race perish. . . .

All the tribes of the north are dancing the war-dance. Two mighty warriors across the seas [Great Britain and France] will send us arms. Tecumseh will soon return to his country. My prophets will tarry with you. They will stand between you and the bullets of your enemies. When the white men approach you, the yawning earth will swallow them up.

Soon shall you see my arm of fire stretched athwart the sky. I shall stamp my foot at Tippecanoe, and the very earth shall shake.

The Indian Removal Policy

In 1830, President Andrew Jackson gave his full support to the Indian Removal Act. Like many frontiersmen, Jackson could have warm friendships with individual Indians but, on a larger scale, he saw Indian societies as an obstacle to the nation's growth and progress. He could also argue that removal was a humane act—a way of preserving the tribes and their cultures.

The selection below is from Jackson's letter to Congress in February 1832.

FROM

President Jackson's Letter to Congress

1832

Washington, February 15, 1832. To the Senate and House of Representatives:

Being more and more convinced that the destiny of the Indians within the settled portion of the United States depends upon their entire and speedy migration to the country west of the Mississippi set apart for their permanent residence, I am anxious that all the arrangements necessary to the complete execution of the plan of removal and to the ultimate security and improvement of the Indians should be made without further delay. . . .

Many of those who yet remain will no doubt within a short period become sensible that the course recommended is the only one which promises stability or improvement, and so it is hoped that all of them . . . will unite with their brethren beyond the Mississippi. Should they do so, there would then be no question of jurisdiction to prevent the Government from exercising such a general control over their affairs as may be essential to their interest and safety. Should any of them, however, repel the offer of removal, they are free to remain, but they must remain with such privileges and disabilities as the respective States within whose jurisdiction they live may prescribe.

The "Trail of Tears"

The removal of the Indians took more than ten years because many of the tribes resisted. Some, like the "Five Civilized Tribes"—the Cherokee, Creek, Choctaw, Chickasaw, and Seminole—had adopted the ways of white society, hoping they would be accepted into the mainstream culture. But the demand for Indian lands was too powerful and tribe after tribe was forced to make the move.

In the following selection, an eyewitness describes a journey of Cherokee on the march the Indians called the "Trail of Tears."

FROM AN

Anonymous Eyewitness Account

1 8 3 9

[We saw a] detachment of the poor Cherokee Indians . . . about eleven hundred Indians—sixty waggons [*sic*]—six hundred horses, and perhaps forty pairs of oxen. We found them in the forest camped for the night by the road side under a severe fall of rain accompanied by heavy wind. With their canvas for a shield from the inclemency of the weather, and the cold wet ground for a resting place, after the fatigue of the day, they spent the night. Many of the aged Indians were suffering extremely from the fatigue of the journey, and the ill health consequent upon it. . . . Several were then quite ill, and an aged man we were informed was then in the last struggles of death.

We met several detachments in the southern part of Kentucky on the 4th, 5th, and 6th of December. The last detachment which we passed on the 7th embraced rising [almost] two thousand Indians with horses and mules in proportion. The forward part of the train we found just pitching their tents for the night, and notwithstanding some thirty or forty waggons were already stationed, we found the road literally filled with the procession for about three miles in length. The sick and feeble were carried in waggons—about as comfortable for traveling as a New England ox-cart with a covering over it—a great many ride on horseback and multitudes go on foot—even aged females, apparently nearly ready to drop into the grave, were traveling with heavy burdens attached to the back—on the sometimes frozen ground, and sometimes muddy streets, with no covering for the feet except what nature had given them.

We learned from the inhabitants on the road where the Indians passed, that they buried fourteen or fifteen at every stopping place, and they make a journey of ten miles per day only on an average.

Refusal to Surrender

Some members of the Cherokee and Seminole nations refused to give in to the removal policy. A few hundred Cherokee retreated into the mountains in Georgia and managed to stay clear of the army and state militia. This small band was never captured; because they stayed in a mountain region, white settlers did not see them as a threat. In 1986, a ceremonial flame was carried from the Cherokee settlements in Oklahoma to Georgia, a symbolic reunification of the people.

In Florida, the Seminoles, led by a courageous chief named Osceola, continued armed resistance for several years. They held off the army for some time, losing hundreds of warriors while the army lost some fifteen hundred men. Most of the Seminoles surrendered and agreed to removal after Osceola was tricked and killed. A few hundred Seminole, along with some escaped slaves, remained free by moving deep into the Everglades, where their descendants still live today.

The Black Hawk War

The last war over Indian lands east of the Mississippi River—the Black Hawk War of 1832—was really a series of raids and ambushes. After several months of bitter warfare, Black Hawk asked for safe passage across the Mississippi for the remnants of his tribe. White settlers ignored his flag of truce and butchered most of the people.

After his capture, Black Hawk was taken to Washington, D.C., and paraded through the streets. Instead of the jeers that military officials expected, huge crowds gathered to cheer him as a brave hero. In the following brief selection, Major Samuel Elliot quotes statements made by Black Hawk during this journey.

FROM

Major Elliot's Journal

1834

"I never knew when the white people came what they wanted. I did not know then [in 1804] that when I touched a quill to a treaty paper, I was giving away the village of my people and all our lands. If anyone had told me that, I never would have agreed.

"Our Rock River home was a beautiful country. I liked my town, my cornfields, and the home of my people. I fought for them."

When [President Jackson] requested [to see] Black Hawk, there was a remarkable meeting between two aging fighters who, while they had never met, had been enemies all their lives. . . . "I am a man," Black Hawk said, "and you are another. I took up the hatchet for my part to avenge injuries which my people could no longer endure. . . . We had no choice but to fight, even knowing we could not win. I will say no more. . . . It is known to you."

PART VI

THE SOUTHERN FRONTIER

Two developments made the history of the South's frontier very different from events in the North. First, Eli Whitney's invention of the cotton gin (a machine for taking seeds out of cotton) in 1792 transformed the South by making cotton the nation's most important cash crop. Southern plantation owners, eager for land, pushed west along the Gulf of Mexico, producing a new tier of territories and states. The rise of "King Cotton" also tied the South more closely to slavery; from 1800 to 1850, the number of slaves doubled, then doubled again to more than four million.

The second important development occurred in the 1820s when a pioneer named Moses Austin received permission from the government of Mexico to settle three hundred American families in the province of Mexico that included Texas. Within fifteen years, a thriving American settlement in Texas fought a revolution that established the independent Republic of Texas.

The Growth of the Cotton Kingdom

While in the South to see about a tutoring job in 1792, a young Yale University student named Eli Whitney heard plantation owners talking about what great value there would be in cotton *if* a way could be found to separate the sticky seeds from the cotton; cleaning the cotton by hand was so slow and tedious that it did not pay to grow it.

Within ten days, Whitney created the first cotton gin (short for "engine")—a simple device that used rotating wire brushes to clean the cotton. ("Gin" was also used as a verb—to gin the cotton.) Using the gin, a worker could clean in one hour as much as ten men could in a full day.

Eli Whitney's patent drawing for the cotton gin, 1794.

Perhaps never in history has a single invention created such sweeping changes in a nation. Plantation owners turned to cotton wherever the land and climate were suitable. The cotton was shipped north to New England and Great Britain, where mill owners were just perfecting large looms powered by water wheels to mass-produce clothing and other fabrics. Suddenly, ready-made clothes were available at very low cost.

The cotton revolution tended to divide America into three interdependent regions: the South, which produced cotton and other crops for the industrial Northeast; the Northeast, which took the South's raw materials and made them into goods like clothing, bedding, curtains, and other fabric items; and the frontier regions of the Northwest, which became the supplier of grain and meat to the other two regions.

In the search for more cotton land, plantation owners pushed westward along the Gulf of Mexico. Rich, black soil—called the "Black Belt"—stretched from Georgia and Florida in the East to

Mississippi, Louisiana, and Arkansas. In the hot, humid climate, owners found they were more dependent on slavery than ever; few freemen, white or black, were willing to work under such conditions.

The following selection provides a glimpse of the new cotton frontier of the South. A northern traveler, Frederick Law Olmstead, describes his travels into frontier Mississippi. (Olmstead was soon to become famous for designing city parks, including New York's Central Park.)

The white population of Alabama and Mississippi increased from 75,000 to more than 200,000 in just four years: 1816–1820.

FROM

Frederick Law Olmstead's Travel Journal

C. 1835

While perfectly aware . . . that [the countryside] bore anything but an appearance of prosperity . . . to a stranger, [the judge] assured me that it was really improving. . . . There were few large plantations, but many small planters or rather farmers, for cotton, thought the principal source of cash income, was much less exclusively an object of attention than in the more southern parts of the state. A larger space was occupied by the maize and grain crops. There were not a few small fields of wheat.

A good deal of cotton was nevertheless grown hereabouts by white labour—by poor men who planted an acre or two, and worked it themselves, getting the planters to gin and press it for them. It was not at all uncommon for men to begin in this way and soon purchase negroes on credit, and eventually become rich men. Most of the plantations in the vicinity, indeed, belonged to men who had come into the country with nothing within twenty years. Once a man got a good start with negroes, unless the luck was much against him, nothing but his own folly could prevent his becoming rich. The increase of his negro property by births, if he took good care of it, must, in a few years, make him independent.

New Orleans: The Cotton Capital

As pioneers moved into the Northwest, New Orleans became the major port for exports of grain and meat. Farmers shipped their produce down the Mississippi River to New Orleans; from there it was shipped to East Coast cities. As the southern frontier opened, the docks and levees of New Orleans were piled high with cotton ready to be shipped to mills in New England or Europe.

LIBRARY OF CONGRESS

John Bachmann's "Bird's eye View of New-Orleans," an 1851 lithograph.

The Lure of Texas

From the 1790s on, Americans had been intrigued by travelers' reports and newspaper accounts of the fertile grasslands and pine forests of eastern Texas. But the land was part of Mexico and, even after Mexico won its independence from Spain in 1822, American settlers were not allowed into the region.

A wealthy merchant named Moses Austin asked the Mexican government to let him bring three hundred families to Texas. Austin's settlers would become Mexican citizens and join the Catholic Church. The government agreed. Although Moses Austin died before he could launch his project, his son Stephen Austin did start the settlement in 1823.

Mexican officials thought that the land purchases and taxes paid by American settlers would be a good source of income. Mexico had just won its independence from Spain and the new nation needed money. At first the Americans kept their part of the bargain, but trouble developed by the early 1830s. Many Americans wanted to build their own churches; they didn't like pretending to be Catholics. Also, when Mexico abolished slavery, officials were not pleased about having to make an exception for Americans who brought slaves, but they felt they could not force the issue.

Stephen F. Austin: The Quiet Founder of Texas

After his father's death, Stephen F. Austin devoted his life to the cause of Texas. He helped lead Texas to independence, but gained nothing for himself. At the age of forty-three, tired and ill, Austin wrote:

> I have no house, not a roof in all Texas that I can call my own. The only one I had was burned at San Felipe during the late invasion of the enemy. . . . I have no farm, no cotton plantation, no income, no money, no comforts. . . . What I have been able from time to time to realize has . . . gone in the service of Texas, and I am therefore not ashamed of my present poverty.

Austin died a few weeks later, on December 27, 1836.

The Alamo

In spite of the conflicts, thousands of Americans flocked to Mexico in the 1820s and 1830s for the fertile soil, inexpensive land, and pleasant climate. Conflict between the newcomers and the government of Mexico was inevitable, however, and by the mid-1830s the Texans were fighting for their independence from Mexico.

The battle at the Alamo became the most famous event in that revolution—and one of the most famous in U.S. history. Sam Houston, commander of the Texas army, did not think that an old mission called the Alamo, near San Antonio, could be held against the large force under Mexico's dictator, General Santa Anna. But Colonel W. Barret Travis, commander of the Texas defenders, was sure they could hold the Alamo until reinforcements arrived. No reinforcements arrived because of delays in getting messages through to other Texans.

The 187 Texans did hold out for 13 days until, surrounded by more than 2,000 Mexicans, they were overwhelmed on March 6, 1836, and every man was killed. "Remember the Alamo!" became the great rallying cry of the Texas revolution and has remained popular ever since.

The first selection below is the appeal of Colonel Travis to "all Americans" to help. The second is from what is claimed to be the journal of Davy Crockett, a famous frontiersman and a former member of Congress. Historians question its authenticity, but it is often included in collections of documents because it is, at the very least, an accurate recounting of events.

ᨏᨏᨏᨏᨏᨏᨏᨏᨏᨏᨏᨏᨏᨏᨏᨏᨏ

FROM

Colonel Travis's Appeal for Help

1836

February 24, 1836

To the People in Texas and All Americans in the World

Fellow Citizens and Compatriots:

I am besieged by a thousand or more of the Mexicans under Santa Anna. I have sustained a continual bombardment and cannonade for twenty-four hours and have not lost a man. The enemy have demanded a surrender. Otherwise the garrison is to be put to the sword if the fort is taken. I have answered the summons with a cannon shot. Our flag still waves proudly from our walls. *I shall never surrender or retreat.*

I call on you, in the name of Liberty, of Patriotism, and of everything dear to the American character, to come to our aid. The enemy are receiving reinforcements daily. I am determined to sustain myself as long as possible and die like a soldier who never forgets what is due to his own honor and that of his country. *Victory* or *death!*

W. Barret Travis
Lieutenant Colonel, Commanding

ᨏᨏᨏᨏᨏᨏᨏᨏᨏᨏᨏᨏᨏᨏᨏᨏᨏ

FROM

Davy Crockett's Journal

1836

February 23, 1836

Early this morning the enemy came in sight, marching in regular order, and displaying their strength to the greatest advantage, in order to strike us with terror. But that was no go; they'll find that they have to do with men who will never lay down their arms as long as they can stand on their legs. . . .

We held a short council of war, and, finding that we should soon be completely surrounded, and overwhelmed by numbers, if we remained in the town, we concluded to withdraw to the fortress of Alamo, and defend it to the last extremity. We accordingly filed off, in good order, having some days before stored all the surplus provisions, arms, and ammunition in the fortress. We have had a large national flag made; it is composed of thirteen stripes, red and white, alternately, on a blue ground with a large white star of five points in the center, and between the points the letters. As soon as all our band . . . had entered and secured the fortress in the best possible manner, we set about raising our flag on the battlements.

March 3

We have given over all hopes of receiving assistance from Goliad or Refugio. Colonel Travis **harrangued** the **garrison,** and concluded by **exhorting** them, in case the enemy should carry the fort, to fight to the last gasp, and render their victory even more serious to them than to us. This was followed by three cheers.

harrangued: argued strongly.

garrison: the men in an army post.

exhorting: urging with a strong argument.

Texas Independence

After the defeat at the Alamo, and another slaughter of Texans at Goliad, many thought the war for independence was over. Morale did not improve when General Sam Houston repeatedly avoided the Mexican army. Finally, on April 21, 1836, Houston was in the battle position he wanted and ordered his troops to attack. The Battle of San Jacinto ended the war and Texas had its independence. Here is part of Houston's report to David Burnet, president of Texas.

The Republic of Texas

The Texans formed the independent Republic of Texas in 1836 and, for the next ten years, appealed to the United States to enter the Union as a new state. The reason it took so long for statehood to be granted was that Texas would enter the Union as a slave state. Another slave state would upset the even division in the Senate between slave-states and free states.

Sam Houston, the hero of Texas independence.

FROM

Sam Houston's Report on the Battle of San Jacinto

1 8 3 6

Colonel Sherman, with his regiment, began the action upon our left wing. The whole line, advancing in double-quick time, rang the war cry, "Remember the Alamo!" They received the enemy's fire and advanced within point-blank shot before our lines fired a single shot.

The conflict lasted about eighteen minutes from the time of close action until we were in possession of the enemy's camp. We took one piece of cannon (loaded), all their camp equipment, their food and supplies, and baggage.

Our cavalry pursued the fleeing enemy to the bridge. Captain Karnes, always the foremost in danger, commanded the pursuers. Many of the troops fought hand to hand. Not having any bayonets, our riflemen used their guns as war clubs.

The rout began at half-past four. The pursuit by the main body continued until twilight. In the battle, our loss was two killed and twenty-three wounded, six of them mortally. The enemy's loss was six hundred and thirty killed; wounded, two hundred and eight; prisoners, seven hundred and thirty.

Sam Houston

Sam Houston was a frontiersman in the mold of Andrew Jackson. Like Jackson, he was tall, possessed a magnetic personality, and had great confidence in his abilities. As a teenager he had lived with an Indian tribe and, at age twenty-four, became a U.S. agent to the Cherokee. When he was thirty, he was elected to Congress and four years later was governor of Tennessee. People considered him the likely successor to President Jackson, but when he divorced his wife the public outcry forced him to resign as governor. He moved to Texas, where he started his new career and became president of the Republic of Texas. He felt that gaining the admission of Texas to the Union in 1846 was his greatest achievement.

PART VII

OPENING THE FAR WEST

The fur trade played a vital role in opening the Far West of the continent. Long before most Americans in the settled East had ever heard of places like Oregon and California, the tough fur trappers known as mountain men were pushing their way through the Rocky Mountains into those coastal lands.

By about 1830, some people in the East became convinced that the trails forged by the mountain men could be used to take wagon trains of pioneers into Oregon and California. The first who tried it, including Christian missionaries, were forced to abandon their wagons, but they proved that the mountain barrier could be breached.

The letters and journals of these trailblazers, and reports given to church groups by missionaries, convinced others to try it. In addition, a few courageous artists went west to see for themselves. Their paintings, drawings, and sketches gave Easterners vivid images of the wonders of the land and the way of life of the the Native American tribes inhabiting the Great Plains, the mountains, and the Pacific coast.

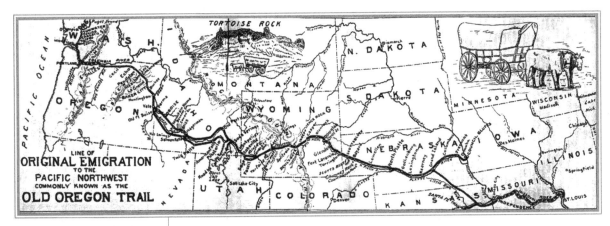

The Old Oregon Trail.

The Mountain Men: Trailblazers of the Far West

Mountain man Jim Bridger.

The mountain men roamed the Rocky Mountains in search of furs, primarily beaver. The pelts brought a high price in the East and in Europe where they were made into men's top hats. Working alone or in small groups, they were tough, independent men who were out of contact with civilization for months at a time. Most had made peace with the Indian tribes, and many had Indian wives, but gunfights with bands of warriors remained common. Each year, the mountain men gathered at a designated place for their "Rendezvous," where they turned in their pelts to the American Fur Company, receiving supplies for the next year as well as money.

As the next selection indicates, the life of the mountain men was violent and dangerous. With their wild pattern of living, many gambled away their earnings before the Rendezvous was over. The selection is from the journal of Samuel Parker, a well-known missionary.

Some of the mountain men, like Jim Bridger, Kit Carson, and Jed Smith, became famous for finding passes through the mountains into California and Oregon. In the second reading, James Beckwourth, a former slave, describes how he found a pass into California.

FROM
Reverend Samuel Parker's Journal
1835

In the afternoon, we came to the Green river, a branch of the Colorado, in latitude 42, where the caravan hold their rendezvous. . . . The American Fur Company have between two and three hundred men constantly in and about the mountains, engaged in trading, hunting, and trapping. These all assemble at rendezvous upon the arrival of the caravan, bring in their furs, and take new supplies for the coming year, of clothing, ammunition, and goods for trade with the Indians. But few of these men ever return to their country and friends. Most of them are constantly in debt to the company, and are unwilling to return without a fortune; and year after year passes away, while they are hoping in vain for better success.

Here were assembled many Indians belonging to four different nations; the Utaws, Shoshones, Nez Perces, and Flatheads, who were waiting for the caravan, to exchange furs, horses, and dressed skins, for various articles of merchandise. . . .

While we continued in this place, **Doct. [Marcus] Whitman** was called to perform some very important surgical operations. He extracted an iron arrow, three inches long, from the back of Capt. Bridger, which was received in a skirmish, three years before, with the Blackfeet Indians. . . . The Doctor pursued the operation with great self-possession and perseverance; and his patient manifested equal firmness. The Indians looked on meanwhile, with countenances indicating wonder. . . . The Doctor also extracted another arrow from the shoulder of one of the hunters, which had been there two years and a half. His reputation becoming favorably established, calls for medical and surgical aid were almost incessant. . . .

The Decline of the Fur Trade

The fur trade did not last many more years. The mountain men were so efficient in their work that they reduced the beaver population close to extinction. Also, by the early 1840s, Chinese silk replaced beaver as the preferred material for men's top hats. The price paid for a beaver pelt dropped from $6 per pelt to $1 by 1845.

Dr. Marcus Whitman led the first overland pioneers into Oregon.

The Hudson's Bay Company

The great rivals of the American mountain men were the trappers working for the British Hudson's Bay Company, which had been formed in 1670. The company controlled the fur trade throughout Canada and the company's governor, George Simpson, vigorously opposed American expansion into Oregon.

Simpson was also one of the West's many colorful characters. He traveled with his entourage in a huge canoe. He always wore a top hat and formal coat as emblems of his authority and had his arrival at every village announced by Scottish bagpipes.

A few days after arrival at the place of rendezvous, and when all the mountain men had assembled, another day of indulgence was granted to them in which all restraint was laid aside. These days are the climax of the hunter's happiness. I will relate an occurrence which took place near evening, as a specimen of mountain life. A hunter, who goes technically by the name of the great bully of the mountains, mounted his horse with a loaded rifle, and challenged any Frenchman, American, Spaniard, or Dutchman, to fight him in single combat. Kit Carson, an American, told him if he wished to die, he would accept the challenge. Shunar defied him. C. mounted his horse, and with a loaded pistol, rushed into close contact, and both almost at the same instant fired. C's ball entered S's hand, came out at the wrist, and passed through the arm above the elbow. Shunar's ball passed over the head of Carson; and while he went for another pistol Shunar begged that his life might be spared. Such scenes, sometimes from passion, and sometimes for amusement, make the pastime of their wild and wandering life.

FROM

James Beckwourth's Recollections

C. 1855

While on this trip [for gold] I discovered what is now known as "Beckwourth's Pass" in the Sierra Nevada. I spotted a place far away to the south that seemed lower than any other. I made no mention of it to my companion. I thought that at some future time I would look into it further. . . .

I stayed a short time in the American Valley. Then I again started out with a prospecting party of twelve men. We went in an easterly direction. All busied themselves in searching for gold. But my errand was of a different kind. I had come to discover what I suspected to be a pass.

It was near the end of April when we entered a large valley. It was at the northwest end of the Sierra range. There were no traces of humans. Our steps were probably the first to mark the spot. We struck across this beautiful valley to the waters of the Yuba. From there we went to the waters of the Truckee. These flowed in an easterly direction, telling us we were on the eastern slope of the mountain range. This slope, I at once saw, would furnish the best wagon road into the American Valley.

On my return to the American Valley, I made known my discovery to a Mr. Turner. He agreed enthusiastically with my views. If I could turn travel into that road, he thought my fortune would be made for life.

James Beckwourth

James Pierson Beckwourth lived with the Crow Indians for a dozen years and was made a chief of the tribe. He could not read or write so he dictated his story to a writer named T. D. Bonner.

Mountain man Jim Beckwourth.

Jim Bridger and Kit Carson

Both Jim Bridger and Kit Carson became famous for finding passes through the mountains, and also for guiding wagon trains and army expeditions. Bridger also built Fort Bridger on the Oregon Trail, providing protection, supplies, and medical help for people heading west. Carson served as a government agent to the Navaho Indians.

Missionaries and the First Pioneers

After the fur traders' Rendezvous described previously, Dr. Marcus Whitman tried to organize the first wagon train to cross the continent to Oregon. To make the event more challenging, Whitman's new bride, Narcissa Whitman, agreed that they could spend their honeymoon on this historic journey. Another couple, Reverend Henry and Eliza Spalding went with them. Although they had to abandon the wagons to get through the mountains, they did make it to Oregon, where they established a medical mission. The Whitmans' letters contributed to a burst of enthusiasm for Oregon—a spirit that became known as "Oregon Fever."

Why Missionaries Led the Way

In 1831 a small group of Indians from two West Coast tribes arrived in St. Louis with an expedition of fur traders. Rumors circulated that the band had come to ask churches in the East to send missionaries to save the souls of their people. A letter in a Christian journal reinforced that notion and it was read from pulpits throughout the East. Dozens of ministers volunteered for mission posts, with most going to Oregon.

FROM

Narcissa Whitman's Diary

1836

June 4, 1836

We have two wagons in our company. Henry and Eliza Spalding and my husband and I ride in one. Mr. Gray and the baggage are in the other. Our Indians [hired as guides] drive the cows. . . .

Our manner of living is far preferable to any in the States [back East]. I never was so contented and happy before. Neither have I enjoyed such health for years. As soon as day breaks, the first we hear is the word, "Arise! Arise!" Then the mules set up such noise as you never heard. This puts the whole camp in motion.

We camp in a large ring. The baggage, men, tents, and wagons are on the outside. All the animals except the cows are fastened to stakes within the circle. This makes watching easier for the guards. They stand watch regularly every night and day to protect our animals. . . .

While the horses are feeding, we get our breakfast in a hurry and eat it. We are ready to start usually at six. We travel till eleven. Then we make camp, rest, and feed. We start again about two and travel until six. . . .

Since we have been in the prairie, we have done all our cooking. When we left, we expected to take bread to last us part of the way. But we could not get enough to carry us any distance. We found it awkward work at first to bake out of doors. Now we do it very easily.

We have tea and plenty of milk. That is a luxury in this country. I never saw anything like buffalo meat to satisfy hunger. We do not need anything else with it. I have now eaten three meals of it, and it tastes good. Supper and breakfast we eat in our tent. We do not pitch it at noon. We have prayers right after supper and breakfast.

Artists' Images of the West

Although the first pioneers began heading for Oregon and California in the late 1830s, the numbers were still small. By 1840, only about two hundred Americans lived in Oregon and even fewer in California. During the 1840s, the numbers joining the wagon trains increased dramatically as people responded to the glowing reports of the first pioneers. In addition to the written reports in letters and journals, the work of artists gave people vivid images of the West, including wonderfully detailed paintings of the landscape, of Indian cultures, and of life on the frontier.

People in eastern cities flocked to the new art galleries to admire the great paintings. Newspapers and magazines had staff artists transform paintings and drawings into **lithographs,** producing a pictorial record available to everyone. A few of the more famous pioneers of western art are presented here; there were a number of others who were less famous and some art remained anonymous.

lithographs: reproductions of paintings created by copying the art onto a metal plate; the plate is then treated so that only the image will hold ink. This technique allowed printers to make multiple copies of a work of art.

George Catlin

Catlin was a Pennsylvanian who trained in the law but soon turned to painting portraits. In the mid-1820s, he was struck by the sight of a procession of western Indians on their way to Washington, D.C. Their quiet dignity impressed him and, suspecting that their way of life would soon vanish, he became determined to record as much of their culture as possible.

Encouraged by his wife, Catlin made several extensive trips west and lived with different tribes, recording their life in paintings, drawings, and in writing. In 1837, he opened an art gallery in New York City, where he displayed 494 paintings of Indian life. Catlin's work in the West extended from 1830 into the 1860s; his writings filled several volumes and are considered an outstanding record of Indian life.

George Catlin, Assinneboine Warrior and His Family, *1861–1869. Catlin's sketches, drawings, and paintings are the only visual record we have of some tribes living in their pre-reservation cultures.*

FINE ARTS MUSEUMS OF SAN FRANCISCO, GIFT OF MR. AND MRS. JOHN D. ROCKEFELLER 3RD, 1979.7.15

George Caleb Bingham,
Boatmen on the Missouri,
*1846. Bingham's paintings
of frontier life became even
more popular in the late
1800s. His use of vivid colors
and careful detail brought
the frontier to life for many
viewers of his work.*

George Caleb Bingham

Beginning in 1840, Bingham produced several outstanding paintings of life on the frontier, especially in the region of the Missouri River. As both a pioneer and an artist he had a sound understanding of life on the edge of civilization. He painted colorful and lively canvases of mountain men, of boatmen on the Missouri, and of frontier town life.

Karl Bodmer

Bodmer was a Swiss immigrant who received formal art training in Europe before coming to America. In the 1830s, Bodmer joined a German prince on a two-year expedition on the upper Missouri River and in the Rocky Mountains. He spent time with such tribes as the Dakota, Mandan, and Ojibway. His paintings of the Mandan, including their dome-shaped houses, were of special importance because the tribe was practically wiped out by a smallpox epidemic in the late 1830s.

NATIONAL ANTHROPOLOGICAL ARCHIVES, SMITHSONIAN INSTITUTION (NEG. NO. 43,175)

Karl Bodmer, Fort Clark
on the Missouri, *February
1834. Many of Bodmer's
drawings and paintings gave
people a sense of the enormous
space of the West.*

Alfred Jacob Miller

On a visit to New Orleans in the late 1830s, Miller met an eccentric Scotsman named Captain W. D. Stewart. Stewart, a veteran of England's wars against Napoleon Bonaparte, still maintained a castle in Scotland. Stewart had Miller accompany him on several excursions into the Rocky Mountains, taking care of all expenses while Miller sketched furiously in pencil and in watercolors. Miller then traveled to Stewart's castle in Scotland to transform the sketches into paintings.

JOSLYN ART MUSEUM, OMAHA, NEBRASKA

Gaining Trust

Artists who wanted to paint Indian life approached the task with respect for the tribe's culture. Catlin, for example, lived with a tribe for several weeks before starting to draw. He knew that, in many tribes, warriors believed they would die if their image was "captured" in a picture.

Alfred Jacob Miller, The Trapper's Bride, *1850.*

Nicholas Point

Father Nicholas Point was a French-born missionary who lived among the tribes of the northern Rocky Mountain region in the 1840s. He completed several hundred paintings and drawings of Indian life. The priest's artwork was stored in a mission building in Montreal and no one knew of its existence until the storage area was opened in the 1970s.

PART VIII

WAGONS WEST!
LIFE ON THE TRAILS

In 1841, a wagon train with sixty-nine pioneers left Independence, Missouri, to follow the Oregon Trail. By 1850, an estimated forty-four thousand had headed west on the same trail. A few of these early expeditions left the road to Oregon to follow one of the trails into California.

That was just the beginning. The westward movement changed suddenly and dramatically when gold was discovered in California in January 1848. Within a few months, "Oregon Fever" was replaced by the "Gold Rush." Thousands of people abandoned farms and businesses to become "Forty-Niners" (the name for gold seekers during that time, because the Gold Rush became strongest in 1849), hoping to find quick riches in the gold fields of Northern California.

The history of the wagon trains extended from the 1830s to the 1880s—a history filled with countless stories of courage and cowardice, heroism and humor, tragedy and triumph. Few epochs in the nation's past have been as well documented as this one—hundreds of men and women kept detailed journals and diaries. They knew that this journey would be the adventure of a lifetime and they wanted to have a permanent record of it.

Getting Started

Horn's Overland Guide to California and Oregon, 1852. The map accompanied Hosea Horn's guidebook and gave Americans a detailed picture of the West. The territories of Oregon, Utah, and New Mexico were soon to be divided into a number of territories and states.

The overland journey began from a "jumping-off" place in Missouri, such as Independence or Saint Joseph, on the edge of the Great Plains. People experienced a sense of excitement and anticipation as they made their way to Missouri. Many traveled there by steamboat or raft, exchanging news and ideas about the journey with other emigrants.

Most families bought their supplies at the jumping-off town, including wagons and livestock. A partylike atmosphere prevailed along the roads as people joined wagon trains or formed their own. In the evening,

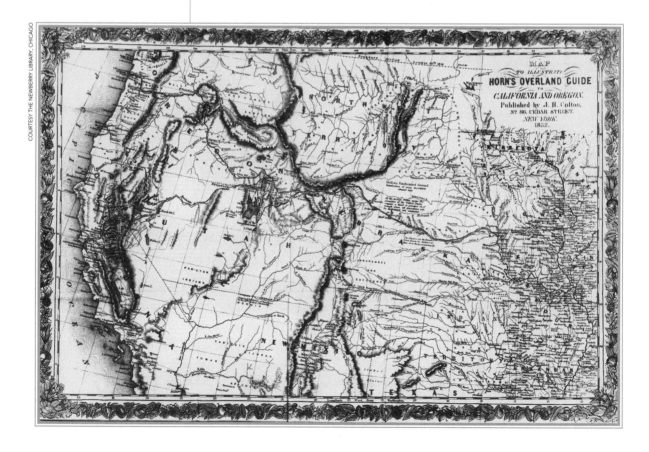

people exchanged visits, wrote last-minute letters, or listened to the music that seemed to come from every camp.

By mid-April, the jumping-off places became crowded because the timing of the journey was critical. Wagon trains could not leave until April or May when the grass was high enough to feed the mules, oxen, horses, and milk cows. They also could not leave too late because snow closed the mountain passes by late October. That meant the emigrants had roughly six months to complete a journey of two thousand miles over land that made it hard to travel twenty-five miles in a day.

The following selection is a description of Independence from Francis Parkman, whose book *The Oregon Trail* became one of the most famous accounts of the westward movement.

St. Louis in the 1850s. From 1800 to 1850, St. Louis was considered America's western outpost. With the opening of the Oregon Trail, Independence and then St. Joseph, Missouri, became the "jumping-off" towns for the wagon trains.

⅏ ⅏ ⅏ ⅏ ⅏ ⅏ ⅏ ⅏ ⅏ ⅏ ⅏ ⅏ ⅏ ⅏ ⅏

FROM

Francis Parkman's The Oregon Trail

1846

At Independence, every store is adapted to furnish outfits—the public houses were full of Santa Fe men and emigrants. Mules, horses, and waggons [*sic*] at every corner. Groups of hardy-looking men about the stores, and Santa Fe and emigrant waggons standing in the fields around.

While I was at the Noland House, the last arrival of emigrants [the ill-fated Donner Party; see page 69] came down the street with about twenty waggons, having just broken up their camp near Independence and set out for the great rendezvous about 15 miles beyond Westport.

What is remarkable, this body, as well as a very large portion of the emigrants, were from the extreme western

Like a Walk in the Park?

As long as the weather was dry, the first part of the journey across the Great Plains was the easiest part. Some reports lured people into thinking the entire distance wasn't all that difficult. An article in the *Missouri Republican* in 1850, for example, claimed that the overland trek was "little else than a pleasure excursion, requiring scarcely as much preparation as a journey from St. Louis to Philadelphia thirty years ago."

Francis Parkman

Parkman was not a pioneer. He went west at the age of twenty-three to study Indian cultures, but his keen sense of human nature turned his work into a wide-ranging account of the many kinds of people who made up the America of the mid-1800s.

When he returned East, Parkman was ill and could not use his eyes to write. He overcame the difficulty by having others read his diary to him and then he dictated large portions of the book. A few years later, he recovered good health and wrote a number of books that have become classics of American history.

states—N. England, sends but a small proportion, but they are better furnished than the rest. Some of these ox-wagons contained large families of children, peeping from under the covering. One remarkably pretty little girl was seated on horseback, holding a parasol over her head to keep off the rain. All looked well—but what a journey before them!

The men were hardy and good-looking. As I passed the waggons, I observed three old men, with their whips in their hands, discussing some point of theology—though this is hardly the disposition of the mass of the emigrants.

I rode to Westport with that singular character, Lieut. Woodworth. He is a great busybody, and ambitious of taking a command among the emigrants. He tells me that great dissensions prevail in their [the Donner Party's] camp—that no organization had taken place, no regular meetings being held—though this is to be done on Saturday and Sunday, and the column to get under weigh [*sic*] on Monday.

Woodworth parades a revolver in his belt, which he insists is necessary—and it may be a prudent precaution, for this place seems full of desperadoes—all arms are loaded, as I have had occasion to observe. Life is held in little esteem.

People in the East pored over magazine illustrations like this one showing wagon train guides setting up camp for the night in 1871.

Free Land

The first pioneers into the Far West believed that the huge tract of land the United States now controlled west of the Mississippi was vast enough that the land would be free. Some people did become "squatters" and simply settled on the land; as more settlers moved in around them, no one bothered to check on the squatters' deeds. With the exception of a few squatters, however, the government soon required some payment for the land. Land speculators often gained title to the land and sold it for far more than the government had required. In 1862 Congress passed the Homestead Act, allowing families to acquire 160 acres virtually free simply by living on the land. Speculators found ways around the new law and managed to control a good deal of the best land. A few years later, Congress granted millions of acres to companies engaged in building railroads.

On the Oregon Trail

Most of the pioneers reached their destination in California or Oregon, but even the successful wagon trains encountered almost daily hardships. In the following selection, Amelia Stewart Knight describes one month of the two thousand-mile trek with her husband, Joel, and their seven children. They began the journey in early April and reached Oregon in mid-September. Even the brief portions printed here suggest the variety of major and minor mishaps that every family faced.

A folk saying on the Oregon Trail: "The cowards never started and the weak die on the way."

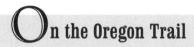

FROM

Amelia Knight's Diary

1 8 5 3

April 16, 1853

Camped last night three miles east of Chariton Point in the prairie. Made our beds down in the tent in the wet and mud. Bed clothes nearly spoiled. Cold and cloudy this morning, and every body out of humor. Seneca [a son, 15] is half sick. Plutarch [another son, 17] has broke his saddle girth. Husband is scolding and hurrying all hands (and the cook), and Almira [daughter, 5] says she wished she was home, and I say ditto. "Home, sweet Home."

18th

Evening—Have crossed several bad streams today, and more than once have been stuck in the mud.

20th

Cloudy. We are creeping along slowly, one wagon after another, the same old gait; and the same thing over, out of one mudhole into another all day.

23rd

All the tents were blown down, and some wagons capsized.

Evening—It has been raining hard all day; everything is wet and muddy. One of the oxen missing; the boys have been hunting him all day. Dreary times, wet and muddy, and crowded in the tent, cold and wet and uncomfortable in the wagon. No place for the poor children.

25th

On our way again, at last, found our cow with a young calf; had to leave the calf behind.

29th

Cool and pleasant; saw the first Indians today. Lucy [daughter, 8] and Almira are afraid and run into the wagon to hide.

May 2nd

Indians came to our camp every day, begging money and something to eat. Children are getting used to them.

5th

We crossed the river this morning on a large steam boat called the *Hindoo,* after a great deal of hurrahing and trouble to get the cattle all aboard. One ox jumped overboard and swam across the river, and came out like a drowned rat.

11th

The men all have their **false eyes** on to keep the dust out.

14th

Wind so high that we dare not make a fire, impossible to pitch the tent, the wagons could hardly stand the wind. All that find room are crowded into the wagons; those that can't, have to stay out in the storm. Some of the boys have lost their hats.

16th

Hard times, but they say misery loves company. We are not alone on these bare plains, it is covered with cattle and wagons.

17th

We had a dreadful storm of rain and hail last night and very sharp lightning. It killed two oxen for one man. We have just encamped on a large flat prairie, when the storm commenced in all its fury and in two minutes after the cattle were taken from the wagons every brute was gone out of sight, cows, calves, horses, all gone before the storm like so many wild beasts. I have never saw such a storm.

[No date]

A few days later my eighth child was born.

false eyes: thin pieces of wood with slits to see through and tied with string or ribbon.

At night, wagons were placed in a tight circle, forming a corral in the middle for oxen, mules, riding horses, and some milk cows.

Glimpses from the Trails

The following selections represent a number of emigrants writing at different times from different trails; the readings will provide at least a glimpse of the variety of experiences that made up life on the overland trails.

The first selection indicates how the letters and diaries of the settlers helped persuade others to make the journey.

How Dangerous Was the Journey?

Walter Prescott Webb in his book *The Great Plains* writes of a government report that estimated that "each mile of the two-thousand-mile journey cost seventeen lives—a total of thirty-four thousand lives." Although there are no precise figures, most historians feel the estimate is accurate.

FROM

Betsey Bayley's Letter

1849

We left Missouri on the 22nd of April and arrived at Chehalem Valley on the 13th of December, all well and hearty, and have been so ever since. Oregon is the healthiest country I ever lived in; there is no prevailing disease, and many people come here for health. The climate is mild and pleasant, and the air pure and bracing. . . . Chehalem Valley is a most beautiful place. It is surrounded with hills, mountains and beautiful groves. We live in full view of Mount Hood, the top of which is covered with eternal snow.

The country abounds in almost all kinds of vegetation. It is one of the best wheat countries in the world. You can sow wheat any time of the year, and you are sure of a good crop. Vegetables do well; cabbage will grow all winter. . . . The country produces all kinds of fruit—whortleberries, blackberries, thimbleberries, strawberries, etc. . . . It scarcely ever snows, and if any snow falls at all it melts quickly. . . . Oregon is settling very rapidly. People are flocking here from all parts of the world.

FROM

Esther Hanna's Diary

1855

[30 miles west of St. Joseph] I think of home and the dear ones there; each day I am getting farther from them. I feel a sadness steal over me at times when I think that I shall see them no more on earth, but it is all for the best.

FROM

Stephen and Mariah King's Letter

1846

You think [the overland trail] is a long road and so it is, but the worst is over when you get started. Be sure and have plenty of flour, that is the main object; start with at least 175 or 200 pounds, and 75 pounds of bacon to the person, fetch no more beds than you want to use, start with clothing a plenty to last you one year after you get here if you have nothing to buy with. . . . Start with at least four or five yoke of cattle to each wagon, young cattle four or five years old are the best. Fetch what coffee, sugar and such things you like—if you should be sick you need them.

FROM

Harriet Ward's Diary

1853

[June 16] This morn some excitement prevailed in our company on account of the discovery of some buffaloes on a high bluff near us. Several of our gentlemen seized guns and ran at full speed, when, Lo! the imaginary buffaloes proved to be holes in the land with weeds growing upon them.

The Nightmare of the Donner Party

In May 1846, one of the largest wagon trains to leave Independence, Missouri, that spring was named the Donner Party, after George Donner, one of the wealthy leaders. Most of them were "tenderfoots"—business people and farmers who knew nothing of travel on the overland trails. Poorly organized and bickering all the way, they made their way to present-day Wyoming. There the wagon train divided, with one group of 89 following George Donner on what was supposed to be a three-hundred-mile shortcut.

The "shortcut" turned out to be a tragic mistake. Trapped by early winter snows in the mountains, the Donner Party experienced one of the great horror stories of the westward movement. The people holed up in scattered cabins, while a few who were strong enough forged ahead, hoping to return with help. Forty-seven of the eighty-two marooned men, women, and children survived—a survival that, for many, depended on eating the bodies of those who had died.

Virginia Reed was thirteen at the time of the horrifying events of the winter of 1846 to 1847. Her stepfather, James Reed, organized the main rescue parties that saved most of the survivors. James Reed had been banished from the wagon train, but his wife, a semi-invalid, and their children stayed with the Donner party; Reed reached California and immediately began organizing rescue teams.

The following excerpts from Virginia's letter to a cousin provide some touching details about the tragedy—and also about the courage and perseverance of those who survived. The selection begins when the family is already trapped by snow high in the Sierra Nevada. (Virginia's unusual spelling has been corrected for easier reading; most of her original grammar has not been changed.)

FROM

Virginia E. B. Reed's Letter

1847

May 16th 1847

My Dear Cousin

. . . We had to go back to the cabin and build more cabins and stay there all winter without Pa. . . . We stopped there the 4th of November and stayed until March and what we had to eat I can't hardly tell you. . . .

[Some of us] dried up what little meat we had and

started out to see if we could get across. . . . We went and was out 5 days in the mountains. Elie give out and had to go back. We went on a day longer. We had to lay by a day & make snow shoes & went on a while and could not find the road & we had to turn back. . . .

We had nothing to eat but ox hides. O Mary I could cry and wish I had what you all at home throw away. We had to kill little Cash the dog and eat him. . . . O my Dear Cousin you don't know what trouble is. . . . We lived on little Cash a week and when Mr. Breen cooked the meat he had left, we would take the bones and boil them 3 or 4 times a day. . .

[Whenever] it snowed and would cover the cabin all over so we could not get out for 2 or 3 days. . . . We had not ate anything for 3 days & we had only a half a hide left and we was on top of the cabin and we seen them [rescuers sent by Reed; they stayed three days for the emigrants to eat and regain some strength].

All of us started out and went a piece but Martha and Thomas give out & so the men had to take them back. Ma and Eliza, James and I went on and o Mary it was the hardest thing yet to come away and leave them there— did not know but what they would starve to Death. Martha said well ma if you never see me again do the best you can. The men said they could hardly stand it. It made them all cry but they said it was better for all of us to go on for if we was to go back we would eat that much more from them. . . .

Some members of the Donner party tried to struggle ahead to find help, but were turned back by the huge snow drifts.

We went over great high mountains as straight as stair steps in snow up to our knees. Little James walked the whole way over all the mountain in snow up to his waist. He said every step he took he was getting nearer Pa and something to eat. Bears took the provisions the men had **cached** and we had but very little to eat. When we had traveled 5 days we met Pa with 13 men headed to the cabins. O Mary you do not know how glad we was to see him. . . .

cached: stored or hid supplies.

Epilogue

Virginia Reed survived her ordeals with no ill effects. She married John M. Murphy in 1850 and lived in San Jose until her death in 1921—seventy-four years after the Donner tragedy.

I have not written you half of the trouble we had but I wrote enough to let you know that you don't know what trouble is. But thank the Good God we have all got through and the only family that did not eat human flesh! We have left [all our possessions] but I don't care for that. We have got through but don't let this letter dishearten anybody and never take short-cuts.

Disturbing News

While the full story of the Donner Party was not known for several years, people in the East heard enough to make them think twice about heading West. A few weeks later, more disturbing news circulated when the Whitman family in Oregon was massacred by Indians. The tribe had been devastated by smallpox and many blamed Dr. Whitman for failing to save them. For a year the number of emigrants declined, but the movement revived quickly with the 1848 discovery of gold in California.

The Mormons

One of the most unusual—and courageous—groups of pioneers were the Mormons, members of a new religious sect. The Mormon Church—officially called the Church of the Latter-day Saints—had been started in 1830 by Joseph Smith (1805–1840) in rural New York State. Smith's magnetic personality and his beliefs, which he said were based on visitations from an angel, rapidly attracted converts—hundreds at first, then thousands. Mormon missionaries traveled throughout Europe, returning with many converts.

Smith and his followers established a remarkably successful community, but wherever they located, they encountered suspicion, hostility, and violence. People resented their clannishness; for example, Mormons regarded all non-Mormons as outsiders and called them "gentiles." The very success of Mormon farms and businesses aroused envy and anger. The most serious charge against them involved polygamy, based on rumors that Smith and other leaders had taken several wives. To many Americans, even though they might be guilty of a sin or two themselves, polygamy seemed to be a great moral offense.

After Smith was murdered by a mob in 1844, leadership fell to Brigham Young, a brilliant, energetic leader whose practical decision making was very different from Smith's more mystical approach. Young led the church to the Great Salt Lake in a dry, barren valley surrounded by rugged mountains in present-day Utah. Young hoped that by moving to land that no one else wanted, the Saints, as they called themselves, could live in peace. They began a settlement called Deseret, which, through hard work and complex irrigation channels, rapidly prospered. The settlement's name was changed to Salt Lake City and the state was renamed Utah before it entered the Union.

In the first selection that follows, one of the Saints offers his view of seeing their new home for the first time before the settlement had been started. The second reading is Brigham Young's view of the area.

A Mormon wagon train.

FROM

William Clayton's Journal

1847

When I commune with my own heart and ask myself whether I would choose to dwell here in this wild looking country amongst the Saints surrounded by friends, though poor, enjoying the privileges and blessings of the everlasting priesthood, with God for our King and Father; or dwell amongst the gentiles with all their wealth and good things

Mormons with Hand Carts

Between 1856 and 1860, three thousand Mormon converts from Europe made the 1,400-mile overland journey to Salt Lake City. Many were unable to afford oxen and wagons, so they carried their belongings in hand carts.

of the earth, to be eternally mobbed, harassed, hunted, our best men murdered and every good man's life continually in danger, the soft whisper echoes loud and reverberates back in tones of stern determination; give me the quiet wilderness and my family to associate with, surrounded by the Saints and adieu to the gentile world till God says return and avenge you of your enemies.

FROM

The Discourse of Brigham Young

1847

We wish strangers to understand that we did not come here out of choice, but because we were obliged to go somewhere, and this was the best place we could find. It was impossible for any person to live here unless he labored hard and battled and fought against the elements, but it was a first-rate place to raise Latter-day Saints, and we shall be blessed in living here, and shall yet make it like the Garden of Eden; and the Lord Almighty will hedge about his Saints and defend and preserve them if they will do his will. The only fear I have is that we will not do right; if we do we will be like a city set on a hill, our light will not be hid.

PART IX

THE GOLD RUSH AND THE MINING FRONTIER

In the spring of 1848, stories and rumors began to drift eastward out of California that gold had been discovered at a place called Sutter's Mill. Efforts to keep the find a secret failed, although the discovery was not verified by the government in Washington, D.C., until September. By then the Gold Rush was on—one of the wildest, zaniest, most exciting exciting episodes in our history.

From all over the country—and the world—thousands of gold seekers headed west, most by the overland trails, some by sailing ship. By 1850 California had enough people to apply for statehood, and by 1852 the population had swelled to more than 200,000. A few prospectors found the fortunes they dreamed of; the great majority did not. Some of the greatest fortunes were made by those who provided the miners with supplies, like food, clothing, and tools.

The Gold Rush not only transformed California, but also speeded up the settling of the West. While thousands of prospectors panned the streams of

California's Sierra Nevada, others were fanning out through the Rocky Mountains and the Great Basin. From the 1850s through the 1870s, strikes of gold, silver, and other metals popped up in present-day Colorado, Nevada, Idaho, Montana, Arizona, and finally the Black Hills of Dakota Territory.

The reading selections in this part describe some of the amazing events in this part of America's westward expansion.

The Discovery at Sutter's Mill

John Augustus Sutter was one of the wealthiest and most powerful men in California in 1848. An immigrant from Switzerland, he had built a fantastic estate of livestock and farms, with a large workforce. After his foreman, James W. Marshall, reported his discovery of gold while working on a mill stream, both men agreed to keep the news secret. They knew that, once the news leaked out, gold seekers would swarm over Sutter's lands and, in their eagerness for gold, would destroy everything he had worked so hard to build. In the following selection, Marshall describes the discovery that changed the course of America's history.

FROM

James W. Marshall's Account

1848

One morning in January 1848, it was a clear cold morning; I shall never forget that morning, as I was taking my usual walk along the **race**, after shutting off the water, my eye was caught by a glimpse of something shining in the bottom of the ditch. There was about a foot of water running there. I reached my hand down and picked it up; it made my heart thump for I felt certain it was gold. The piece was about half

race: a human-made channel to direct a flow of river water to a mill wheel; the turning wheel then provided enough power to run machines.

the size and of the shape of a pea. Then I saw another piece in the water. After taking it out, I sat down and began to think right hard. I thought it was gold, and yet it did not seem to be of the right color; all the gold coin I had seen was of a reddish tinge; this looked more like brass. I recalled to mind all the metals I had ever seen or heard of, but I could find none that resembled this. Suddenly the idea flashed across my mind that it might be iron pyrites. I trembled to think of it! This question could soon be determined. Putting one of the pieces on hard river stone, I took another and commenced hammering it. It was soft and didn't break; it therefore must be gold. . . .

While we were looking in the race after this discovery, we always kept a sharp lookout, and in the course of three or four days we had picked up about three ounces—our work still progressing as lively as ever, for none of us imagined at that time that the whole country was sowed with gold.

About a week's time after the discovery I had to take another trip to the fort; and to gain what information I could respecting the real value of the metal, took all we had collected with me and showed it to Mr. Sutter, who at once declared it was gold, but thought with me, it was greatly mixed with some other metal. . . . After hunting over the whole fort and borrowing from some of the men, we got three dollars and a half in silver, and with a small pair of scales we soon cyphered it out that there was no silver nor copper in the gold, but that it was entirely pure.

This fact being ascertained, we thought it our best policy to keep it as quiet as possible till we should have finished our mill, but there was a great number of soldiers in and about the fort, and when they came to hear of it, why, it just spread like wildfire, and soon the whole country was in a bustle.

So there, stranger, is the entire history of the gold discovery in California—a discovery that hasn't as yet been of much benefit to me.

Two Gold Rush Victims: Sutter and Marshall

John Sutter's suspicion that his Fort Sutter estate would be damaged by gold seekers was quickly realized. Within a year, prospectors had trampled over his fields and streams, setting up camps, digging and panning for the precious metal, even consuming or driving off his cattle. While Sutter had always helped pioneer wagon trains and had campaigned for statehood, he was officially a Mexican citizen and the new California state government refused to acknowledge his ownership of the lands.

By 1853, Sutter was broke. He spent the rest of his life trying to have his lands restored. He died in Washington, D.C., in 1880. Marshall, too, did not gain from the discovery and soon was forced off the Sutter lands by the mobs of prospectors. Although he later received a small state pension as a pioneer in creating the state of California, he gained nothing from the Gold Rush.

California Gold Fever

Mining camps with colorful names like "Hangman's Gulch" appeared overnight near a strike; they usually disappeared just as quickly when the strike "played out."

America had never witnessed anything like the California Gold Rush. It began in the spring of 1848 and gained so much momentum the next year that all of the gold seekers became known as "Forty-Niners." The earliest prospecters who swarmed over the mountains and valleys north of Sacramento had the best chance of finding gold—and they did find some surprisingly rich veins. The best year was probably 1852, when nearly $81 million in nuggets and gold dust were taken out. The largest nugget was found in 1854, weighing 141 pounds.

The prospectors created hastily built tent and wood villages, with names like Poker Flat, Grub Hollow, and Red Dog. Most of these settlements were abandoned as the gold supply dwindled. By 1860, large corporations moved in with heavy machinery and explosives. They quickly

gained control of the gold fields; by that time, most of the surface gold had been found and nearly all of the gold seekers had drifted away.

The selections that follow include prospector John Clark's account of the crowded overland trails and the problems created by so many wagon trains, and a newspaper correspondent's account of the impact of the Gold Rush on San Francisco.

FROM
John Hawkins Clark's Journal
1852

May 7.—It took [nearly] all day to put up our wagons, adjust the harness, break the oxen, store away our provisions in the different vehicles of transportation, count out the cooks, drivers and train master. . . . About six miles from camp to the high lands through a wilderness of woods, mud and water. After a hard day's work through mud knee deep we pitched our tents upon high land near a spring of good water and wood in abundance. . . .

May 8.—Bright was the morning and light our hearts as we rolled out of camp on this, our first day's journey of 2,000 miles. . . . As far as the eye can reach the road is filled with an anxious crowd, all in a hurry. Turned out at twelve o'clock to let our teams to grass, which was quite abundant all along the line of our day's travel. One o'clock we are again on the move. . . . Camped at six o'clock; wood and water to carry some distance, but plenty of good grass. . . .

May 14.—Camped last night on the bank of the Nemaha river, and this morning were called upon to bury a man who had died of cholera during the night. There have been many cases of this disease, or something very much like it; whatever it may be it has killed many persons on this road already. . . .

There are many camps on the banks of this river; many are sick, some dead and great numbers discouraged. I think a great many returned from this point; indeed, things look

The Magic of Gold

In July 1850, there were 526 ships in San Francisco Harbor, plus 100 or more in the river towns like Sacramento. In those first two or three years, many of the miners had a lot of money to spend in the city. Some were bringing in $300 to $500 a day for weeks at a time; a few were panning up to $5,000 a day.

alkalai: a bitter, salty chemical that poisoned watering holes.

a little discouraging and those who are not determined may waver in their resolution to proceed. . . .

May 26.—Out early this morning, and our pathway now lies in the valley of the magnificent Platte river. . . .

Fort Kearney lies five miles from our camp, and while marching towards it this morning it presented quite an interesting appearance; but, on a near approach, the charm we felt on first seeing it gradually faded, and when we arrived on the spot, found instead of clean looking buildings, a number of rusty looking houses without paint or whitewash. A postoffice, hotel and store are located here; a smith shop is free to all who have cause to use it—a great convenience to many. . . . Many sick immigrants are taken to the hospital and treated by the army surgeons—and people without money are frequently assisted. . . .

June 23.—From this point to the topmost heights of the Rocky Mountains is our next stage of travel. . . . The road becomes crooked, rough and flinty; the face of the country a broken mass of natural ruins. . . .

This is the land of the mirage, of "delusions," of the sage brush, and the **alkali** waters; a land of wonders and of hardships; a land to be avoided or left behind as soon as possible. Saw many dead cattle on the road; the poisonous water and the great scarcity of feed begins to tell on the poor brutes. . . .

Aug. 18.—To-day we make the last grand effort of this wearisome trip; this is considered the hardest bit of travel on the route, and consequently more preparation is made for the journey. We have grass and water on board for our teams which is now universally carried, the distance about forty miles. . . . About ten miles out the dead teams of '49 and '50 were seen scattered here and there upon the road. Very soon, however, they became more frequent and in a little while filled the entire roadside; mostly oxen, here and there a horse and once in a while a mule. Wagons, wagon irons, ox chains, harness, rifles and indeed all the paraphernalia of an emigrant's "outfit" lay scattered along this notorious route, reminding one of the defeat of some great army.

Sailing Options

The greatest American sailing ships were called clipper ships—large ships that carried acres of sail that sped the ships smoothly and swiftly across the seas. While clipper ships carried hundreds of prospectors to San Francisco, many gold seekers took slower, cheaper journeys to present-day Panama or Nicaragua, then hiked across the narrow Isthmus to the Pacific Coast where other ships, some of them barely seaworthy, carried them to California.

Flying Cloud, one of the most famous of the clipper ships, made the voyage from New York around South America to San Francisco in just eighty-nine days. That record was never broken by a three-masted sailing ship. The era of the beautiful clipper ships was very short—the billowing white sails were replaced by faster steam-powered ships beginning in the 1860s.

San Francisco in 1850. San Francisco was a town of three thousand when the Gold Rush began. Within less than two years it "boomed" to a city of more than twenty thousand.

The Remarkable Dame Shirley

Louisa Clappe was a lovely but frail Victorian lady when she arrived in California in 1851. Her husband, Fayette Clappe, was sickly, and Louisa described herself as a "half-dying invalid." But they headed to the gold boom town of Rich Bar and she began to write. Her articles, called "The Shirley Letters," became popular in newspapers and were reprinted in several eastern publications as well. She wrote about the colorful life at "the

Mining cradles and Long Toms, 1853. Earth and water were shoveled into a box-shaped cradle or into a long trough called a Long Tom. By "rocking the cradle" the gold-bearing sand sank to the bottom; the sand was then washed in a pan and the gold nuggets or dust picked out.

Panning for Gold

Dame Shirley's description of mining with a "Long Tom" was also called "placer mining," referring to the deposits of gravel and sand shoveled into the trough. Miners still "panned" for gold, swishing sandy water round and round until the heavy gold settled to the bottom. Prospectors found it very difficult to stand in ice-cold streams for more than an hour or two in order to pan. The pan was used to get the gold out of the "riffle box" or to test a placer deposit.

digs," including the violence: "In the short space of 24 days, we have had murders, fearful accidents, bloody deaths, a mob, whippings, a hanging, an attempt at suicide and a fatal duel." Because of her fame and her personal dignity, the miners called her "Dame Shirley," a title associated with English nobility.

As the gold played out in late 1852, Dame Shirley decided it was time to leave and she found she hated to go. "And only think," she wrote, "of the shrinking, timid, frail thing I used to be. I have become a strong woman. I like the wild and barbarous life. I go from the mountains with a deep sorrow. . . . Here, at last, I have been contented."

In this selection she describes the basic technique of mining gold.

F R O M

Louisa Clappe's The Shirley Letters

1 8 5 1

In many places the surface-soil, or in mining phrase, the "top dirt," "pays" when worked in a "Long Tom." This machine, (I have never been able to discover the derivation of its name,) is a trough, generally about twenty feet in length, and eight inches in depth, formed of wood, with the exception of six feet at one end, called the "riddle," which is made of sheet-iron perforated with holes about the size of a large marble. Underneath this collander-like portion of the "long-tom," is placed another trough, about ten feet long, the sides six inches perhaps in height, which divided through the middle by a slender slat, is called the "riffle-box."

It takes several persons to manage, properly, a "long-tom." Three or four men station themselves with spades, at the head of the machine, while at the foot of it, stands an individual with a shovel. The spadesmen throw in large quantities of the precious dirt, which is washed down to the "riddle" by a stream of water leading into the "long-tom" through wooden gutters or "sluices." When the soil reaches the "riddle," it is kept constantly in motion by the man with the hoe.

Of course, by this means, all the dirt and gold escapes through the perforations into the "riffle-box" below, one compartment of which is placed just beyond the "riddle." Most of the dirt washes over the sides of the "riffle-box," but the gold being so astonishingly heavy remains safely at the bottom of it. When the machine gets too full of stones to be worked easily, the man whose business it is to attend to them throws them out with his shovel, looking carefully among them as he does so for any pieces of gold, which may have been too large to pass through the holes of the "riddle." At night they "pan out" the gold, which has been col-lected in the "riffle-box" during the day.

Panning for gold.

The Real Gold-Rush Fortunes

Some of the greatest fortunes to emerge from the Gold Rush were amassed by merchants who supplied the needs of the Forty-Niners. Four of these men—Mark Hopkins, Collis Huntington, Charles Crocker, and Leland Stanford—were from rural New York State; they joined the Gold Rush but, instead of mining, they opened stores in Sacramento. All four did well by selling food and tools to the miners. In the 1860s, they pooled their modest fortunes and their skills to build the nation's first transcontinental railroads. Known as California's "Big Four," all established great fortunes and played major parts in developing California.

Another great fortune was created by Levi Strauss. He used tent canvas to make durable pants that the miners called "Levi's." As the business grew, he added blue dye and reinforced the corners of the pockets with rivets. Levi's rapidly became popular with cowboys as well as miners and soon became standard work pants throughout the country.

Women at the Mining Camps

In this section, a popular gold field author describes life in the mining camps, where more than 90 percent of the population was male. "Old Block" was the pen name of Alonzo Delano. His stories, which he called "Pen-Knife Sketches," were very popular in the "diggings" (mining towns) and then found a wide audience in the East.

FROM

Old Block's Pen-Knife Sketches

1853

Women were scarce in mining camps, but some managed to make better money than their husbands by washing clothes or cooking.

COURTESY CALIFORNIA STATE LIBRARY

The fact that women are so rarely seen in the diggings is attested to by the following true story.

Early one Sunday morning our mess was awakened by the discharge of a musket near our heads. Jumping up we exclaimed:

"What's the matter? What has happened?"

"'What's the matter!'" shouted the **stentorian** voice of one of our neighbors, "turn out, turn out; new diggins, by Heaven! A live woman came in last night!"

We knew that delays were always dangerous, so shouldering our picks and shovels, pistols and rifles . . . we marched to the new tent . . . and gave three cheers and a discharge of firearms. The alarmed occupants rushed to the door to see what was up. Our captain mounted a rock, and addressed the amazed husband in something like this strain:

"Strangers—We have understood that our mothers were women, but it is so long ago since we have seen them, that we have forgotten how a woman looks, and being told that you have caught one, we are prospecting to get a glimpse."

stentorian: extremely loud.

The man, a sensible fellow, by the way, entering into the humor of the joke, produced the lovely *creature* he had caught.

The Mining Frontier Moves East

Beginning in the late 1850s, the news of gold strikes echoed through the Rocky Mountains and the Great Basin. In addition to gold, prospectors were finding rich veins of silver, copper, and other metals. Thousands of California miners headed east, where they were known as "Yondersiders," while "Greenhorns," from the other direction, became part of the westward movement.

From present-day Arizona and Colorado in the South to Montana and the Dakotas in the North, "boom towns" grew up overnight. Some quickly became ghost towns, and a few developed into permanent cities, like Denver, Colorado and Virginia City, Nevada. The mining frontier brought thousands of new settlers to the West and new territories were organized throughout the mining region. By the 1870s, the open frontier was largely limited to the Great Plains.

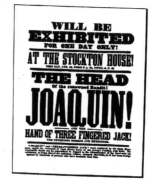

When a posse supposedly killed a notorious bandit named Joaquin Murieta, they toured California in 1853 with the pickled head in a whiskey jug. Some people called it a fraud and, in fact, no evidence was ever found to prove Murieta existed. Some said the bandit was not one man but five!

Stagecoaches and the Pony Express

From the 1850s to the end of the century, the stagecoach became one of the most common sights throughout the West. The main line, from St. Louis to San Francisco, was started by John Butterfield in the late 1850s. With nearly two hundred relay stations stretched over the twenty-eight-hundred-mile route, Butterfield's drivers could deliver mail and passengers in twenty-five days. The line used brightly painted Concord wagons (made in Concord, New Hampshire).

But westerners were eager for faster delivery of urgent mail and, before 1861, there was no telegraph service. The result was the short, colorful reign of the Pony Express, which started in April 1860. Riding day and night in relays, the Pony Express riders carried small mail packets from St. Joseph in Missouri to San Francisco in the remarkable time of just ten days. However, the completion of the first telegraph line in October 1861 marked the beginning of the end of the Pony Express.

"Go West, Young Man, Go West"

In 1851, a newspaper editor named John B. L. Soule wrote those words in a newspaper, the *Terre Haute* [Indiana] *Express*. Horace Greeley, well-known editor of the *New York Tribune*, was so impressed by the enthusiastic editorial that he printed the entire piece in the *Tribune*. Although Greeley gave full credit to Soule, people ever after associated the phrase with Greeley.

A Pony Express rider racing past workers installing the transcontinental telegraph line.

The following two selections describe the colorful, romantic eras of the Pony Express and the stagecoaches as the "cars of the desert".

"Old Charley" Parkhurst

One of the most famous drivers of stagecoaches and Wells Fargo freight wagons was known as "Old Charley" Parkhurst. He survived countless scrapes with hostile Indians and outlaws, and travelers felt safer when Parkhurst held the reins or "rode shotgun" next to the driver. Not until Parkhurst's death in 1879 was it discovered that Charley was a woman.

FROM

Mark Twain's Roughing It

1 8 7 2

We had a consuming desire, from the beginning, to see a pony-rider, but somehow or other all that passed us and all that met us managed to streak by in the night, and some heard only a whiz and a hail, and the swift phantom of the desert was gone. . . . But now we were expecting one along every moment, and would see him in broad daylight. Presently the driver [of Twain's stagecoach] exclaims: "Here he comes!" Every neck is stretched further, and every eye strained wider. Away across the dead level of the prairie a black speck appears against the sky, and it is plain that it moves. . . . In a second or two it becomes a horse and rider, rising and falling, rising and falling—sweeping toward us nearer and nearer . . . and the flutter of the hoofs comes faintly to the ear—another instant a whoop and a hurrah from our upper deck, a wave of the rider's hand . . . and man and horse burst past our excited faces, and go winging away like a belated fragment of a storm!

FROM A

St. Joseph Newspaper Account

1865

The whips crack, and the two cars of the desert go rolling forward, each stage pulled by six sleek horses. Across level plains, over hills, and down steep winding canyons our horses leaped at their utmost speed. One route of eight miles we traveled in thirty minutes! . . . We spent only seventy-two hours upon the five hundred and seventy-five miles of desert between Salt Lake, and Virginia City, Nevada. . . .

Reaching Austin on the last 400-mile leg of our journey, our vehicle whirled around the last street-corner, ran for several yards poised upon two wheels, while the others were more than a foot from the ground, but righted again; and with this neat finishing stroke, ended our ride of four hundred miles accomplished in fifty-one hours.

Stagecoach Passengers

Men and women who rode a stagecoach two thousand miles from St. Louis, Missouri, to Sacramento, California, had a unique experience. They paid $600 for the twenty- to twenty-five-day journey crammed into one of the three leather upholstered benches with eight other people. There were only two major stops every twenty-four hours when they could eat a fairly decent meal, stretch their legs, and maybe wash off the alkalai dust. In spite of all the hardships, most travelers found the journey to be a rewarding one, especially for the outstanding scenery they passed every day.

Pony Express Facts and Figures

The Pony Express lasted only nineteen months but has always loomed large in the nation's history as a symbol of the American frontier spirit. Each rider averaged 75 miles, changing horses every 10 to 15 miles. There were 25 "home stations" where riders were changed, and 190 relay stations for changing horses. The average age of the "expressmen" was 19; William F. Cody (later known as Buffalo Bill) was 15 when he rode for the Pony Express and David Jay was 13. The young men dressed lightly, their only weapons a revolver and a knife. The mail was written on thin, lightweight paper at a cost of $5 per half-ounce (later lowered). They traveled a total of 650,000 miles and carried 34,753 pieces of mail, losing only one mail pouch. The 2,000-mile trip usually took 10 days; a record of 7 days and 17 hours was set in March 1861 to carry President Lincoln's inaugural address to California. In October 1861, a telegraph was sent in a few minutes from New York to San Francisco over the first telegraph line, which stretched 3,500 miles. That marked the end of the Pony Express.

Two Great Writers

The mining frontier launched the writing careers of two great American writers: Bret Harte and Mark Twain (the pen name for Samuel Clemens). Both men emerged as writers of the West in 1861, working on newspapers first in Nevada, then in California. It was while working on the Virginia City, Nevada, *Territorial Enterprise* newspaper that Clemens changed his name to Mark Twain. Mark Twain was a term used on steamboats to call out the depth of the water. It was also in the West that Twain wrote "The Celebrated Jumping Frog of Calaveras County," a tale that gave him modest fame throughout the country and launched his literary career.

Bret Harte was a friend of Mark Twain and a fellow newspaper writer in California. He became famous for his short stories about life in the mining camps. His stories, such as "The Luck of Roaring Camp" and "The Outcasts of Poker Flat," provided a wealth of colorful details. His style, which also influenced Mark Twain's writing, became known as "local-color realism" and was widely imitated by writers throughout the country in the late 1800s.

PART X

FROM SEA TO SHINING SEA

The year 1846 became known as the "Year of Decision" in America's history. Within the space of a few months the nation added thousands of square miles to its territory when the government annexed—or took over—what had been the Republic of Texas; persuaded Great Britain to end a long boundary dispute by signing a treaty that granted Oregon and present-day Washington to the United States; and entered a war with Mexico that ended in 1848 with America in possession of California, Colorado, Arizona, New Mexico, and parts of several other states.

These acquisitions changed the map of North America even more than the Louisiana Purchase had in 1803, adding more than one million square miles. To many Americans, this expansion was not only natural but inevitable. The feeling had been growing for years that the nation was destined for greatness.

They believed that the United States, which had been a small, struggling nation huddled along the Atlantic Coast when the century began, would soon extend from the Atlantic to the Pacific—"from sea to shining sea."

In 1845, a New York newspaper editor named John L. O'Sullivan provided a name for this expansionist mood—"Manifest Destiny." "It is our manifest destiny," O'Sullivan wrote, "to overspread and possess the whole continent which Providence has given us for the great experiment of liberty and self-government."

The readings in this part will provide some insights into America's expansion in the 1840s.

Polk and Manifest Destiny

When James K. Polk was elected president in 1844, he was determined to expand the nation's boundaries in all directions. He promised that his first step would be the annexation of Texas. That prize was denied him, however, when the outgoing president, John Tyler, completed annexation three days before leaving office.

Polk then set his sights on Oregon and California. When Mexico refused to sell California, the United States used a border dispute to initiate a war with Mexico.

The Mexican leaders overestimated the strength and fighting ability of their forces. The Americans launched a three-pronged invasion of Mexico while other army and navy groups moved into California. The Mexican troops fought ferociously, but they could not match the weaponry or the shooting skill of the Americans, as the following reading suggests. The battle described involved a small American force called "Doniphan's Thousand." Colonel Alexander Doniphan commanded a regiment of Missouri mounted volunteers. They marched some thousand miles across present-day New Mexico and deep into Mexico itself. William H. Richardson, an officer of the regiment, wrote the diary quoted here. After sixteen months of such one-sided battles, Mexico surrendered.

FROM
The Diary of William H. Richardson
1 8 4 6

In the union of our forces we are one thousand strong. . . . After marching 12 miles, we came to Bracito, and encamped at 10 o'clock. We stripped our horses as usual, and picketed them out; went out to hunt wood to cook our dinners. Some of the men had gone at least a mile from camp when the alarm was given, *"to arms! to arms! . . .* We saw a cloud of dust as if the whole of Mexico was coming down upon us.

"Throw away your wood and bring your horses into camp," an officer commanded. We found our Orderly at his post, directing the men to load their guns and get into line. Every man was at his proper place in a few minutes. By this time the Mexican army was in sight, and had formed a battle array at a distance of a mile from us. . . .

We were ordered to march double time to open ground on the left. Our captain told us to reserve our fire till the enemy was in fair rifle distance, and added that he hoped no man in his command would act the coward. . . . He had scarcely done speaking, when the enemy commenced firing at us. . . . They advanced closer and continued to advance, pouring in volley after volley, till the sound of bullets over our heads reminded me of hail. We waited impatiently for the word of command. It was finally given: "Fire!"

One loud peal of thunder was heard from our Missouri rifles. Bewilderment and dismay was the result, for, thrown into confusion, the Mexicans moved away to our left. Another volley, well aimed, caused them to retreat towards our wagons, where they were met by a round from a wagon company. . . . The Mexican loss was estimated at thirty or forty killed and 50 wounded, while we had but two slightly wounded.

Victory and the Slavery Issue

General Winfield Scott led the largest American force that invaded Mexico by sea. Although the forces were often outnumbered by three or four to one, the result of every battle was like the one described in William H. Richardson's diary. Scott's fourteen thousand men took Mexico City in the autumn of 1847 and the war was over.

In the Treaty of Guadalupe Hidalgo, Mexico was forced to turn over roughly one-third of its territory—California and the huge areas known as Utah Territory and New Mexico Territory.

Many Americans were not pleased with the war. They knew that the South would demand the right to extend slavery into parts of the new lands. A young Illinois Congressman named Abraham Lincoln was defeated for reelection because he had opposed the war. Others were upset because the Native Americans and Mexicans living in the territory had no voice in the new government; the Mexicans, in fact, suddenly found themselves unwelcome residents in a foreign society.

In the following selection, Frederick Douglass, former slave and famous leader of the antislavery movement, expresses a view shared by many African Americans.

Wartime Losses

The war with Mexico cost America four thousand wounded and thirteen thousand dead—but more than eleven thousand died from disease or accident.

FROM

Frederick Douglass's The North Star

1848

In our judgment, those who have all along been loudly in favor of a vigorous prosecution of the war, and heralding its bloody triumphs have no sincere love of peace. . . . Had they not succeeded in robbing Mexico of the most important and most valuable part of her territory, many of those now loudest in . . . favor of peace would be loudest and wildest for war—war to the knife.

Our soul is sick of hypocrisy. . . . That an end is put to the wholesale murder in Mexico is truly just cause for rejoicing; but we are not the people to rejoice; we (all Americans) ought rather . . . hang our heads in shame, and, in the spirit of profound humility, crave pardon for our crimes at the hands of a God whose mercy endureth forever.

West Point: Training Ground for Generals

In the years leading to the war with Mexico, Congress had come very close to closing the United States Military Academy at West Point. The nation did not seem to need a special training school for army officers. The experience of the Mexican War made Americans grateful for the institution. The volunteers were largely untrained and unruly. West Point officers provided not only discipline, but also the leadership that made victory possible. Some young officers, like Robert E. Lee, Ulysses S. Grant, Thomas Jackson, and George Thomas, became outstanding generals in the Civil War.

The Bear Flag Republic

In June 1846, a band of about thirty Americans rode into the town of Sonoma, told the local Mexican official that California was now an independent republic, and raised a homemade flag featuring a picture of a bear. This Bear Flag Republic lasted about a month. When Navy Commodore John Sloat sailed into Monterey Bay and raised the U.S. flag, claiming California for the United States, the Bear Flag Republic ceased to exist.

The Fate of the Native Americans

The huge area of land acquired from the war with Mexico was home to thousands of Native Americans, divided into many different tribes. The U.S. Army had only about fifteen thousand men to protect white settlers in this area and in Oregon Territory. In 1851, in an effort to establish peaceful relations with the many tribes, the government held peace talks near Fort Laramie (in Wyoming Territory). About ten thousand Indians camped near the fort as their leaders agreed to the government's offer: each of the tribes would allow free passage for the wagon trains across their territory and would be limited to a certain region of the bison migration routes as their hunting grounds. In return, the government would distribute $50,000 worth of supplies to the tribes each year.

This peace effort was bound to fail. Few Indians understood the details of the Fort Laramie Treaty, and the white people, especially the miners, ignored the treaty boundaries. In addition, the agents signed to distribute the supplies often cheated the Native Americans and sold much of the food and other supplies assigned to them. By the mid-1850s bands of Indian warriors began raiding wagon trains, stealing horses and cattle, or demanding money for allowing the pioneers to cross Native American lands. This was the start of more than two decades of warfare, pitting the outnumbered U.S. cavalry against the increasingly desperate tribes.

A second Fort Laramie treaty was signed in 1868. The Sioux chiefs agreed to a "Great Sioux Reservation" covering all of present-day South Dakota. Pictured here are Spotted Tail, Roman Nose, Old Man Afraid of His Horses, Lone Horn, Whistling Elk, Pipe, and Slow Bull (from left to right). Despite this new treaty, the bloodshed continued.

The Civil War, 1861–1865

One of the issues that led eleven states of the South to try to leave the Union of States and form an independent Confederate States of America involved the expansion of slavery into the new lands of the West. People in the South feared that the more populous North would soon control all branches of government and force the South to free its more than four million slaves. This fear led to the belief that, by extending slavery westward, new states could be formed where slavery was allowed. Since each new state would have two senators, the North could not gain control of the Senate. The course of the war—as well as the causes and the results—are detailed in American Heritage® American Voices, *Civil War and Reconstruction.*

Almost-Free Land

Throughout the Civil War years, pioneers and gold seekers continued to follow the westward trails. The government encouraged this movement with the Homestead Act in 1862, granting any citizen or immigrant the right to 160 acres of public land simply by living on the land for five years.

FROM

The Homestead Act

1862

(U.S. Statutes at Large, Vol. XII, p. 392 ff.)

AN ACT to secure homesteads to actual settlers on the public domain.

Be it enacted, That any person who is the head of a family, or who has arrived at the age of twenty-one years, and is a citizen of the United States, or who shall have filed his declaration of intention to become such, as required by the naturalization laws of the United States, and who has never borne arms against the United States Government or given aid and comfort to its enemies, shall, from and after the first of January, eighteen hundred and sixty-three, be entitled to enter one quarter-section or a less quantity of unappropriated public lands, upon which said person may have filed a pre-emption claim, or which may, at the time application is made, be subject to pre-emption at one dollar and twenty-five cents, or less, per acre; or eighty acres or less of such unappropriated lands, at two dollars and fifty cents per acre, to be located in a body, in conformity to the legal subdivisions of the public lands, and after the same shall have been surveyed: Provided, That any person owning or residing on land may, under the provisions of this act, enter other land lying contiguous to his or her said land, which shall not, with the land so already owned and occupied, exceed in the aggregate one hundred and sixty acres.

PART XI

RAILROADS AND CATTLE DRIVES

Probably no single event had a greater effect on the West than the completion of the railroad that linked the east and west coasts of America. The transcontinental railroad led to the largest westward migration of settlers; it also contributed to the destruction of the bison herds and an end of the free, roaming life of the western Native Americans. The readings in this part will show how the railroad led to the great, colorful era of the cowboy, the cattle drives, and what people think of as the "Wild West."

The First Transcontinental Railroad

In 1860, the United States had more than thirty thousand miles of railroad—all of it east of the Mississippi River. The ease and speed of railroad transportation in the East was a marked contrast to the horse-and-wagon travel in the West. In 1862, Congress approved funds for the first transcontinental railroad. There were actually two railroads. The Union Pacific would start at Omaha, Nebraska, and build westward; the Central Pacific Railroad built eastward from Sacramento.

The building of this railroad was a remarkable feat of engineering and construction. Although some beginnings had been made, the real construction was not underway until the Civil War ended in 1865. The selections here describe the Chinese immigrants who worked on the Central Pacific; work on the Union Pacific by Irish immigrants and others; and the meeting of the two lines at Promontory Point, Utah, in May 1869.

From Bret Harte's Tribute, 1869

What was it the Engines said,
Pilots touching—head to head
Facing on the single track,
Half a world behind each back?

"Hell on Wheels"

As the railroads inched along, overnight towns sprang up to meet the workers' needs. These short-lived settlements, with a gambling hall, a store, and a saloon, were called "Hell on Wheels."

FROM

The Alta California

1868

When the first blue-clad Chinese workers appeared at the roadbed of the Central Pacific, the muscular Americans laughed at them because they looked so small and frail. They quickly proved their worth and Mr. [Charles] Crocker has wisely hired thousands, even sending to China itself for recruits.

We have witnessed their great efficiency in cutting through snowdrifts fifty feet high. They have been lowered in baskets 2,000 feet down cliffs to hand-drill holes for blasting powder. We have been told of their work in carving tunnels through mountains—fifteen tunnels in all, the longest measured at 1,659 feet. Above all, these pigtailed coolies, drinking their hourly tea brought to them in buckets, have gained the respect of everyone.

FROM
The New York Daily Tribune

1868

Mr. [Grenville] Dodge, the Chief Engineer of the Union Pacific, has forged more than 8,000 workers—many of them Irish immigrants—into a formidible army. They have fought off the depredations of Cheyenne war parties, although dozens of the workers have been brutally scalped. . . . A train of 24 cars is needed to supply this army its daily needs. Each train is shunted onto a siding when a fresh supply train comes through.

Five men work on each 700-pound iron rail, ten men to a pair of rails. Thirty seconds is allowed for each pair of rails, two rail lengths every minute, three blows to each spike, 10 spikes to the rail; that means 400 rails, 4,000 spikes, and 12,000 hammer blows for a single mile of track!

FROM
The New York Daily Tribune*'s Front Page*

MAY 11, 1869

Promontory Summit, Utah, May 10—The last rail is laid! The last spike, the golden one, driven! The Pacific Railroad is completed!

The point of junction is 1,086 miles west of the Missouri River, and 600 miles east of Sacramento City.

The Golden Spike

After the ceremony joining the two railroads, workers moved in and took out the last tie and the golden spike. The laurel-wood tie was destroyed in the 1906 San Francisco earthquake and fire. The golden spike is kept at Stanford University. Printed on it are the dates of the groundbreaking and the completion, the names of the officials, and a prayer: "May God continue the unity of our Country as this Railroad unites the two great Oceans of the world."

The joining of the rails at Promontory Point, Utah, in 1869.

The "Guests of the Golden Mountain"

When news of the California Gold Rush reached China, thousands of young Chinese men headed for California, intending to stay only long enough to get rich as "guests of the Golden Mountain." Only a few struck it rich, but many stayed and opened laundries, restaurants, and other businesses. In spite of prejudices against Asians, they also sent to China for their wives or girlfriends or for mail-order brides and formed thriving communities.

Crossing the Continent in Comfort

The Railroad Age

By 1870, the nation's railroad mileage had nearly doubled to 59,000 miles—and that was just the beginning. By 1890, the nation had more than 165,000 miles of railroad track, as four more transcontinental lines were built, as well as dozens of shorter connecting lines.

In 1884, to improve train scheduling, the American Railway Association divided the United States into the four time zones we continue to use today: Eastern, Central, Rocky Mountain, and Pacific. Within each zone, clocks were set at the same time. In the past, each town set its own time, so there might be a dozen time changes in a single day's travel.

Thousands of emigrants had crossed the land from the Mississippi to the Pacific Coast by walking most—or all—of the way alongside their plodding wagon trains. Smaller numbers, but still in the thousands, had died in the attempt or had turned back, disheartened. Then, suddenly, the miracle of the railroad made it possible for people to glide over the landscape in six days rather than six months. The journey was not very comfortable for those with the cheapest seats, but it was swift. And builders like George M. Pullman designed dining cars, "sleepers," and parlor cars that transformed trains into hotels on wheels. A *New York Times* reporter described this new chapter in the westward movement.

FROM

The New York Times

1870

Crossing the Great Plains, where the level ground allowed the mighty engine to reach full speed, we covered *twenty-seven miles in twenty-seven minutes,* while in the new dining cars, champagne glasses filled to the brim, spilled not a drop. After dinner, the passengers gathered in the drawing-room car—or parlor car, as some prefer to call it—to sing hymns with an organ accompaniment, while the train, with its great, glaring . . . eye, lighting up long vistas of prairie, rushed into the night and the Wild. Then to bed in luxurious coaches: where we slept the sleep of the just and only awoke the next morning . . . at eight o'clock, to find ourselves at the crossing of the North Platte, three hundred miles from Omaha—*fifteen hours and forty minutes* after we left it.

Cowboys and Cattle Drives

In the 1500s, early Spanish settlers had introduced longhorn cattle into the grasslands of Mexico and Texas. Some of the cattle escaped and developed into wild herds. These herds grew at a phenomenal rate, especially after 1800, and by the time of the Civil War (1861–1865), more than five million longhorns were roaming free over the grasslands of the southern plains.

Cattle ranchers knew that a steer, costing about $2 to round up, would be worth almost $40 at market in an eastern city like New York or Philadelphia. The problem was how to get the cattle to those markets, because the distance was so great. The transcontinental railroad offered a solution and a handful of pioneer cattlemen forged trails north to meet the railroad.

These cattle trails opened the exciting, colorful era of the cowboy and produced many of our images of the "Wild West." The long, slow, and dangerous cattle drives lasted only a short time, from the 1860s to the late 1880s. The selections that follow will provide glimpses of cowboy life and the hazards of the trails: a fifteen-year-old cowboy describes a night stampede; another tells of the special danger of not finding water; and future president Theodore Roosevelt, himself a rancher in the mid-1880s, provides a sketch of the cowboy personality.

A cowboy trying to turn stampeding cattle, from a painting by famed western artist Frederic Remington.

Finding Markets

The ranchers found three major outlets for their cattle. The largest market was reached by driving a herd to a rail head, like Abilene or Dodge City; the steers were then loaded onto cattle cars and shipped to meat-packing plants in Chicago or to cities farther east. Some cattle owners took their herds to the mining towns in the Rocky Mountains. The third large market was the Indian reservations, where the government was required to provide meat for the tribes.

Improving Quality

Many people in the East complained that the meat of the longhorns was tough and stringy. By the 1870s, ranches were mixing the longhorns with shorthorn cattle, like Herefords, often buying herds from settlers in Oregon and driving them to ranches in Montana, or Wyoming Territories.

FROM

Cowhand Jim McCawley's Account

1887

On the third night, as usual, I was on the first guard, just Scandalour John [the nickname of cowhand John E. McCanless] and me, and about nine o'clock a black cloud from the northwest come up. I had on my slicker, or oil coat. It began to rain in torrents. The vivid lightning began to flash. The thunder began to roar. And all at once the steers got on their feet and in less time than it takes to tell it they was gone. The night was as dark as ink, only for the lightning. My horse was on his job, so he stayed with the cattle. Then I realized that the so much talked of stampeding herd of longhorn steers was now a reality. Every time it would lighten and a loud clap of thunder follow they would change their course, and in a short time I found the herd had split or divided, but into how many bunches I didn't know. After some two hours of storm the rain quit and soon it cleared off and the moon shined out, but I didn't know where my pard was or which way the wagon might be.

I had about three hundred head of steers and after everything was still they lay down and I thought I'd see if I could find the other part of the herd. But to my sorrow, I could not, so I thought I'd shoot my six-shooter and see if anybody would come or answer me. Bang she went and away went the bunch I was holding. Now I had more trouble than if I had a let things alone. After chasing them for an hour, I guess, I got them stopped, but I didn't shoot any more. Well, the moon in all its beauty came at last, and as the sun arose across the eastern horizon in all its glory, [there] never was a [more worn out] sleepier boy than I was. But still I was in trouble, for there I was with a bunch of cattle all alone with nobody in sight and I didn't know which way to go to the wagon. I was so hungry and tired I didn't know what to do.

About ten o'clock a man came in sight. They was looking for me but didn't know which way to look. He told me the direction the wagon was. I lit out. I had drifted something like ten miles to the southeast and if any boy ever did enjoy something to eat it was me. If bacon and beans ever tasted good it was then. The boys all told the boss he had lost his tenderfoot, but when they found out I had held a bunch all night they didn't say tenderfoot any more.

༄ ༄ ༄ ༄ ༄ ༄ ༄ ༄ ༄ ༄ ༄ ༄ ༄ ༄

FROM

Andy Adams's Account

1 8 6 6

[Adams's outfit, moving two thousand longhorns, had to cross a stretch of eighty miles without water.]

Good cloudy weather would have saved us, but in its stead was a sultry morning without a breath of air, which bespoke another day of sizzling heat. We had not been on the trail over two hours before the heat became almost unbearable to man and beast. Had it not been for the condition of the herd, all might yet have gone well; but over three days had elapsed without water for the cattle, and they became feverish and ungovernable. The lead cattle turned back several times, wandering aimlessly in any direction, and it was with considerable difficulty that the herd could be held on the trail. The cattle congregated into a mass of unmanageable animals, milling and lowing in their fever and thirst. . . . We threw our ropes in their faces, and when this failed, we resorted to shooting; but in defiance of the **fusillade** and the smoke they walked sullenly through the line of horsemen across their front. Six-shooters were discharged so close to the leaders' faces as to singe their hair, yet, under a noonday sun, they disregarded this and every other device to turn them, and passed wholly out of our

A Cowboy's Equipment

A cowboy's clothing and equipment were designed for function, not for appearance. Everything in his gear had a purpose—usually several purposes. The broad-brimmed hat worn on the southern plains was an umbrella in the rain, shade against the sun, a hood against the cold when the sides were tied about the ears, and a drinking gourd for cowboy and horse. The cowboy's saddle was his workbench, heavy and durable. The pommel, or saddle horn, was bolted to the "tree"—the wooden frame, or foundation—making a solid post for roping a steer. The cantle (back) was high to give the rider a firm seat when the horse climbed steep hills. Wooden stirrups covered with leather protected the foot from being crushed against the sides of cattle. All other pieces of equipment—like chaps, boots, and kerchief—were also practical and, like all the equipment, were adapted from the original Spanish cowboy, or vaquero.

fusillade: many guns firing at once or in rapid succession.

Cowboy Slang

flea trap: a cowboy's bedroll

hot rock: a biscuit

necktie party: a hanging

eating gravel: being thrown from a horse

maverick: a steer (or horse) with no brand

Rocky Mountain mocking-bird: a donkey

biscuit shooter: the trail cook

control. In a number of instances wild steers deliberately walked against our horses, and then for the first time a fact dawned upon us that chilled the marrow in our bones—the herd was going blind.

FROM

Theodore Roosevelt's Autobiography

1885

Cowboys include wild spirits of every land, yet the latter soon become indistinguishable from their American companions, for these plainsmen are far from being so heterogeneous a people as is commonly supposed. On the contrary, all have a certain curious similarity to each other; existence in the West seems to put the same stamp upon each . . . of them. Sinewy, hardy, self-reliant, their life forces them to be both daring and adventurous, and the passing over their heads of a few years leaves printed on their faces certain lines which tell of dangers quietly fronted and hardships uncomplainingly endured.

Nat Love, also known as "Deadwood Dick," the most famous of the black cowboys.

© BETTMAN/CORBIS

African American Cowboys

As many as one-third of the cowboys were either Mexican Americans or African Americans, including blacks who had escaped from slavery. The most famous black cowboy was Nat Love, who had been born into slavery in Tennessee but was freed during the Civil War. "It was the great West I wanted to see," Love wrote. "The wild cowboy, prancing horses of which I was very fond, and the wild life generally, all had their attractions for me." When the long drives ended, he became successful as a rodeo rider.

The Wild West: Fact and Fiction

Along the western frontier, there was usually a gap between the first settlement and the establishment of law and order. At times this gap was
filled with a running conflict between law enforcement officers and the
lawless. In cattle towns, like Abilene and Dodge City, the lawlessness was
created by fun-loving cowboys. After several hard, dreary weeks on the
trail, the cowboys delivered their herd and then wanted to "cut loose."
Their wild celebrations sometimes got out of hand. After a year or two, as
a town became more prosperous, the citizens would no longer put

*A poster advertising a book
filled with "facts" about some
of the Wild West's best-known
characters.*

up with rowdy behavior. They
would then hire enough deputies
to help the sheriff establish order,
or they might form a vigilance
organization.

Mining towns also had their
reckless days, which often lasted
several years because the mountain towns were so isolated. The
first of the following selections
describes lawlessness and vigi-
lante justice in Montana Territory. The second reading is about
one of the most famous lawmen,
Wild Bill Hickok. Like many
outlaws and lawmen, Hickok's
reputation was far grander than
his actual exploits. Writers for
eastern newspapers, magazines,
and "dime novels" embellished
every escapade they could find,
turning cheap crooks into notorious gunmen, and mediocre
sheriffs into heroic good guys.
The Hickok episode, for example, represents the only time he
killed a man.

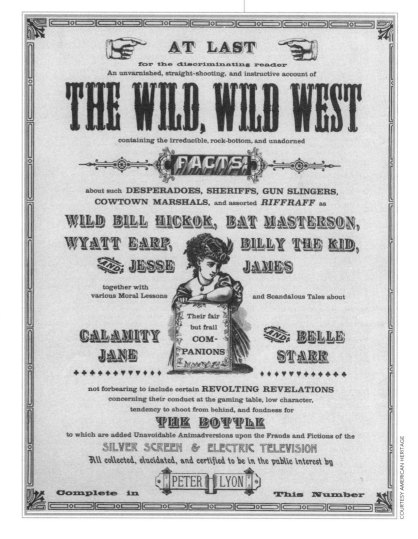

FROM

John W. Clampitt's Account

1889

The wonderful discoveries at Alder Gulch of the almost fabulous wealth of placer diggings attracted . . . a large number of the dangerous class, who saw a broad and rich field for their lawless operations.

To illustrate the class of **desperadoes** engaged in this **nefarious** work, we will take the case of Henry Plummer, a man of such smooth manners and insinuating address that he was termed "a perfect gentleman," although known to be both thief and assassin. . . .

Plummer, who had been chosen chief of the **"Road Agents"** Band, had likewise succeeded in having himself elected sheriff of the county and appointed two of the "band" his deputies. And all this in spite of his well-known character. One of the sheriff's deputies was an honest man, and becoming too well versed in the doings of Plummer and associates was sentenced to death by the road agents, and publicly shot by three of the band.

There was no longer any security of life or property. Men dared not go outside of Virginia [City] after dark, nor risk their lives by informing upon those who had robbed or wounded them on the highway. Inhuman murders occurred each day. . . .

A man sentenced to be whipped for larceny . . . offered to inform upon the road agents. He was met soon after by one of their number, George Ives, in open daylight on a public road . . . and shot to death. . . .

The sight of this man's body, brought into town . . . stirred . . . the honest men of the community. . . . A party of citizens . . . scoured the country, surprised accomplices of the murderer, and obtained from them the unwilling confession that George Ives was the murderer. By the following evening he was captured and taken . . . into Nevada City.

desperadoes: dangerous men or women; bandits.

road agents or *highwaymen* were bandits whose specialty was holdups, especially robbing stage coaches and their passengers.

nefarious: evil; infamous.

He was given a trial. The bench was a wagon; the jury twenty-four honest men; the aroused citizens stood guard with guns in hand while the trial proceeded, with their eyes fixed upon the desperadoes who had gathered in force to aid, support, and if possible to rescue their comrade in crime. Counsel was heard on both sides, reliable witnesses proved the prisoner guilty of numerous murders and robberies. Condemned to death, his captors repressed every attempt at rescue. . . . Amid the . . . murderous threats of the assembled ruffians the condemned assassin . . . was led to a gallows upon which he **expiated** his **manifold** crimes.

The next day the far-famed Vigilantes of Montana were organized. . . . Their work was sure; their retribution swift; their power prodigious. The Vigilance Committee became as terrible to the outlaws as they themselves had formerly been to the honest . . . part of the community.

Plummer . . . was seized, and . . . was executed on a Sunday evening . . . on a gallows which he himself had erected.

The Vigilantes . . . assumed the duties of captors, judges, jurors, and executioners. But they were not guilty of excesses. . . . In no case . . . was a criminal executed without evidence establishing his guilt.

expiated: to make up for; to atone for.

manifold: varied; many different kinds.

FROM

John W. Clampitt's Account of Wild Bill Hickok

1889

There were a lot of tall tales about Wild Bill Hickok, but through it all a couple of facts stand out: First, he was a crack shot—both with a six-gun and a carbine. In fact, as a lawman in Abilene, he rarely had to draw his guns to make an arrest; by giving occasional demonstrations of his marks-

Wild Bill Hickok, by N. C. Wyeth, c. 1904. Hickok was called the "fastest gun in the West." As a lawman, he rarely had to draw his gun because his reputation was enough to keep the peace. (He died after being shot in the back while playing cards.)

COURTESY THE ADAMS MUSEUM AND HOUSE COLLECTION

manship, he made sure no one was likely to challenge him. He had also been a courageous scout during the Civil War. . . . The newspapers have credited him with killing as many as 36 men during his tenure as a lawman in a number of towns, but these numbers belong in the dime novels. However, the crucial event took place in Abilene on October 5, 1871. Hickok was called to quell a disturbance near the train station. A tavern owner named Phil Coe drew on Wild Bill. Coe fired first, his bullet going harmlessly through Hickok's coat.

Hickok fired and hit Coe in the gut. "I've shot too low," someone heard him say. He then heard someone behind him. Turning, he saw a figure moving in the shadows. Without thinking Hickok fired, accidentally killing his deputy who was also his friend.

Shaken by the tragedy, Hickok left law enforcement. He wandered through the West, spent some time with Buffalo Bill's Wild West Show, and devoted most of his time to gambling. In August, 1876, he was in Deadwood, Dakota Territory, a rough miner's town. Playing poker, he never saw a drifter named Jad McCall come up behind him; McCall killed him with a single shot.

The End of the Cowboy Era

Many people thought the booming cattle business would continue for years. Teddy Roosevelt, from his Dakota ranch in the 1880s, saw the end coming, as indicated in the first of the following selections. By the mid-1880s, more and more farmland was being fenced in by barbed wire.

Then came the winter of 1886–1887, as described in the newspaper report reproduced as the second selection.

FROM

Theodore Roosevelt's Autobiography

1885

The free, open-air life of the ranchman, the pleasantest and healthiest life in America, is from its very nature ephemeral. The broad and boundless prairies have already been bounded [with barbed wire] and will soon be made narrow. It is scarcely a figure of speech to say that the tide of white settlement . . . has risen . . . like a flood; and the cattlemen are but the spray from the crest of the wave, thrown far in advance, but soon to be overtaken. . . . The great fenceless ranches . . . will be . . . divided into corn land, or else into small grazing farms where a few hundred head of stock are closely watched and taken care of.

FROM

The New York Sun

1888

The blizzards that began last November [1887] started the horror and then, in January, the plains were struck by the most devastating snowstorm in the memory of the oldest fur traders. When the range was open [in past years] the cattle could move ahead of the snow, finding . . . or pawing for . . . enough grass to survive. Riding the fence lines today, however, this correspondent was saddened by the sight of hundreds of starved and frozen cattle leaning against the barbed wire that halted their movements. With temperatures sinking to minus seventy degrees (Farenheit) and the snow shoulder deep, they could not have survived even had the barbed wire been absent. . . .

Cattlemen tell me that the winter has claimed nine out of every ten cattle on the open range. . . . The days of the open range are gone forever.

PART XII

THE LAST INDIAN WARS AND THE CLOSING OF THE FRONTIER

As America's westward expansion swept across the Great Plains and the mountains, what became of the estimated 250,000 Indians who had roamed this vast area, many of them following the huge herds of bison? Consider the life of Sitting Bull, a great chief of one branch of the Sioux.

He was born about 1831 in a camp on the northern plains and became a wise and respected leader of the Sioux. His name was Tatanka Iyotake but the whites called him Sitting Bull.

When Sitting Bull was growing up, he watched the first wagon trains inching cross the Sioux hunting grounds. By the time he became a chief, the long cattle drives were moving north to meet the railroads, which sliced east-west across the hunting grounds of several tribes. When Sitting Bill was about forty years old, gold was discovered on Indian lands in Dakota territory, and the invasion of thousands of white gold seekers led many of the Plains tribes to vote for war.

Sitting Bull led the Sioux to two of their few victories, both in 1876, at the battles of the Rosebud and the Little Bighorn. But the westward movement was already entering its final phase—the settling of the Great Plains. Before 1870, pioneers had crossed over that enormous grassland as rapidly as possible because they thought the prairie was too dry for farming and the sod too thick to plow. In just twenty years, from 1870 to 1890, a new wave of pioneers changed this unwanted land into one of the world's greatest farming regions.

Soon after the 1876 victories, Sitting Bull saw that warfare could not hold back the tidal wave of settlers. He led a small band to Canada, then returned and moved onto a reservation in Dakota Territory. In December 1890, he was mistakenly shot and killed by reservation police. That same year, the U.S. Census Bureau announced that there was no longer a line that could be called a frontier; in other words, the frontier was closed.

Settlers in Sod Houses

Advantages and Disadvantages

A soddy's greatest advantage may have been its low cost. A family could build a good one, complete with a couple of glass-paned windows, for under $5. The sod made good insulation, too, keeping the interior cooler in summer and easy to heat in winter.

The great disadvantage was that you never knew what might drop out of the sod roof onto your dining table, such as bits of sod, various bugs, and an occasional snake.

Several innovations made it possible for pioneer families to farm the grasslands of the Great Plains. In the 1830s, for example, John Deere invented a "chilled steel" plow that could easily slice through the thick prairie sod. At the same time, Cyrus McCormick developed machines for harvesting wheat that made it possible to harvest enormous wheatfields with a few workers. Other developments helped, like strains of wheat from Turkey that could survive the bitter cold prairie winters. In addition, railroads brought settlers west, often selling them land at a low price, and carried farm products to eastern markets.

The Homestead Act of 1862 allowed settlers to claim 160-acre spreads as long as they lived on the land and improved it by building a house or farming it. The first pioneers on the Great Plains headed for the river valleys, where there were trees as well as water. Later settlers found only treeless grassland, so they devised dwellings out of sod—the thick, matted grasses that build up over many years and reached a depth of four feet or more. These dwellings, called "soddies," are described in the following selection by Charles Reed, son of a pioneer.

FROM

Charles Reed's Description

C. 1868

The first step was to "break" the ground, which was done by turning the sod over with a "breaking plow." . . . The moldboard of a breaking plow consisted of three curved rods that turned the sod over grass side down, instead of a solid metal plate. . . .

Pieces of sod used in building were usually about three inches thick, twelve inches wide, and thirty inches long. . . .

The mechanics of building a sod house were fairly simple, but it required good workmanship to put up a good one. . . . The first tier of sod was laid grass side down on the virgin ground site. If the building space was not level, the lower corners were built up by sod so that the upper tiers of sod in the wall would be level. . . .

Early Nebraska sod houses had half-length windows . . . that didn't move up or down. The window opening in the sod wall was shaved off just enough to allow a one-sash window frame to be inserted and then the cracks around the window would be chinked up with mud or home-made plaster. For a door you placed upright boards on both sides of the door opening, installed a sill board at the bottom, and a cross brace at the top. Then a plain slat door was made and hung on ordinary barn hinges.

A sod house, c. 1895. The most expensive item in a sod house like this was the glass-paned window, usually bought through a mail-order catalog.

Bison, Horses, and a Way of Life

Sioux Chief Sitting Bull.

A Prediction

In 1853, a Delaware chief named Black Beaver made this prediction: "The time is not far off when the vast herds [of bisons] will be only a memory. Deprived of their means of subsistence, the . . . Indians will become the scourge of the civilization that hems them in, and they in their turn will have to be exterminated."

Some of the tribes of the Great Plains, like the Cheyenne and the Black-foot, had originally lived in the East, until pushed westward by the pressure of white settlement. Others, like the Sioux and Crow, had lived on the prairie for years. All of these tribes had become expert horsemen, riding the tough little prairie "ponies," descended from horses that had escaped from the Spanish many years earlier. The Indians gave up farming and lived by hunting the huge herds of bison that roamed the Great Plains from Canada to Mexico. The herds by 1850 were estimated to number as many as fifty million animals. The two readings in this section describe the hunting and fighting skills of the Plains Indians.

FROM

George Catlin's Account

C. 1836

Amongst their feats of riding, there is one that has astonished me more than anything of the kind I have ever seen . . . in my life: a strategem of war, learned and practiced by every young man in the tribe; by which he is able to drop his body upon the side of his horse at the instant he is passing, effectually screened from his enemies' weapons as he [lies] in a horizontal position behind the body of his horse, with his heel hanging over the horse's back. . . . In this wonderful condition, he will hang whilst his horse is at fullest speed, carrying with him his bow and his shield, and also his long lance of fourteen feet in length, all or either of which he will wield upon his enemy as he passes; rising and throwing his arrows over the horse's back, or with ease and equal success under the horse's neck. . . .

A Sioux, even firing from horseback can drive an 18-inch arrow completely through the neck of a bison. In warfare, according to U. S. Army Colonel Hastings, an Indian on horseback has no [equal] in fighting ability. An Army trooper must reload after each shot. During that time his Sioux opponent can fire a total of eight arrows.

An Indian warrior using his horse as a shield, from a painting by Frederic Remington.

FROM

Captain Alexander Stewart's Letter

1844

The Indians of the grasslands are not only extraordinary horsemen but they are also remarkable warriors. War, in fact, is a favorite occupation, second only to hunting the shaggy bison, but it is rarely the kind of warfare we associate with the spectacle of **Waterloo.** The Indians will fight battles **en masse,** but only when they feel trapped by whites or become engaged in a feud with another tribe. Their preferred form of warfare is to raid an enemy's camp either for stealing ponies or for counting *coup* [from the French word for a blow].

Counting *coup* involves nothing more than touching an enemy, either with the hand or with a special piece of wood called a *coup* by sneaking up on the enemy or by riding brazenly into a heavily armed camp, touching an enemy, then racing out again. A warrior is much more proud of adding eagle feathers to his war bonnet for the *coups* he has accomplished than for a dozen enemy scalps, because each *coup* is a symbol of courage.

New Firepower

In the late 1840s, U.S. Army soldiers began to receive Samuel Colt's revolvers—handguns that fired six shots before reloading. Americans could finally match the firepower of warriors with bows and arrows.

Waterloo: The last battle of the wars of the French emperor Napoleon versus the British when two huge armies met on the field of battle.

en masse: with a large army instead of individually or in small war parties.

The Bison Supermarket

At the height of the hunting season, Plains Indians might take only the choicest cuts of meat from a kill, but they also used the bison to meet a great many needs in addition to food. The hides were used for making tepee coverings, clothing, moccasins, arrow quivers, bags, shields, and drums. Horns were used to make tools or decorations, the bones were turned into knives, war clubs, and smaller items, even dice, and muscles and sinews proved useful as laces or bindings.

The End of the Bison Herds

When the wagon trains were crossing the Great Plains in the 1840s and 1850s, the pioneers were awed by the enormous herds of bison they saw. A stampeding herd made the earth tremble for miles and for the herd to pass a given point might take six or seven hours. Within a generation, the bisons had almost completely disappeared.

The tragic end of the bison herds began in the early 1870s after eastern tanneries had developed ways to turn the hides into leather. At nearly the same time the railroads arrived in the West and it was the railroads, more than any other factor, that destroyed the bison to the edge of extinction. The railroad companies hired professional hunters, such as William "Buffalo Bill" Cody, to shoot bison. Some of the animals were used for hides or to feed the railroad workers, but most were left where they were killed. (Cody killed more than four thousand bison in one stretch of eighteen months.) As the herds disappeared, so did the Indian way of life. The next two selections describe the incredible slaughter of the North American bison.

Vanishing Buffalo

In 1872, the U.S. Commissioner of Indian Affairs saw the slaughter of the buffalo as a mark of progress. He wrote, "The Northern Pacific Railroad will of itself . . . leave the ninety thousand Indians ranging between the two transcontinental lines as incapable of resisting the Government as are the Indians of New York or Massachusetts."

By 1900 the herds had been reduced from more than fifty million bison (some estimates are as high as seventy-five million) before whites came to fewer than one thousand.

FROM

George Ramspert's Account

1881

A company, with teams, saddle-ponies, ammunition, and provision . . . make a headquarters camp. . . . From the camp, the team follows the hunter [who] has a big cartridge-rifle, usually a 100-grain Sharpe which . . . can carry [up to] two miles. . . . When he sees a herd he crawls . . . within shooting distance, and shoots down the leader. The herd will not fly without a leader; and by the time they have a new one, [the hunter] is ready and downs him. Watching his chances and being a good shot . . . he sometimes succeeds in getting down fifty or sixty buffaloes. . . . Their bellowing is almost deafening; it is enough to terrify an inexperienced hunter. . . . When the herd leaves, the skinners move in. . . .

When the wagons are well loaded they head for camp to unload the hides and stretch them out to dry. Several hundred hides being sometimes stretched out at one camp, it presents quite an attractive scene.

FROM

William Webb's Buffalo Land

1872

During certain periods in the spring and fall, when the large herds are crossing the Kansas Pacific Railroad, the trains run for a hundred miles or more among countless thousands of the shaggy monarchs of the plains. The bison has a strange and entirely unaccountable instinct or habit which leads

breech-loaders: rifles that could be loaded rapidly.

putrefaction: rotting.

wantonly: wastefully.

Railroad passengers and crewmen shooting bison from a train. A single train like the one pictured might leave three or four thousand dead animals behind.

it to attempt crossing in front of any moving object near it. . . .

When the iron-horse comes rushing into their solitudes . . . instead of fleeing back to the distant valleys, away they go, charging across the ridge over which the iron rails lie, apparently determined to cross in front of the locomotive at all hazards. . . . Hence it often happens that the cars and the buffalo will be side by side for a mile or two. . . . During these races the car windows are opened, and numerous **breech-loaders** fling hundreds of bullets among the densely crowded and flying masses. Many of the poor animals fall and more go off to die in the ravines. The train speeds on, and the scene is repeated every few miles until Buffalo Land is passed. . . .

Let this slaughter continue for ten years, and the bison of the American continents will become extinct. . . . All over the plains, lying in disgusting masses of **putrefaction** along valley and hill, are strewn immense carcasses of **wantonly** slain buffalo. They line the Kansas Pacific Railroad for 200 miles.

The Last Indian Wars

As the bison herds rapidly diminished, the bewildered tribespeople were left with two unhappy choices: facing hunger, they could lay down their weapons and move onto the reservations the government had set aside for them; or they could unite several tribes and fight for their lands.

The government established a "peace policy" aimed at forming treaties with the tribes and moving them onto large reservations, where the government would provide food, clothing, and farming tools, as well as schools. In return, no outsiders would be allowed on Indian lands. The 1868 Medicine Lodge Treaty, for example, promised that no one but tribal members "shall ever be permitted to pass over, settle upon, or reside" in the Black Hills of the Dakotas. When gold was discovered in the Black Hills in 1874, however, miners flocked to the hills. Bands of furious Sioux warriors started steady warfare against the white settlements and the army. Army officials felt that their first duty was to force the Indians back onto the reservations. The warfare, which had started ten years before the Medicine Lodge Treaty, became fiercer in the mid-1870s. In 1876, Native Americans won their greatest victory at the Little Bighorn River; it was also to be their last victory in what people called the "Indian Wars."

The battle came about when General George Armstrong Custer led a force of six hundred cavalry into Sioux land in Minnesota Territory. Although his scouts warned him that an estimated eight thousand Sioux and Cheyenne (including up to three thousand warriors) had joined forces, Custer ignored their reports. He was already a well-known figure, a bold officer in the Civil War who was sometimes in trouble with his superiors for acting on his own. He had also angered President Ulysses S. Grant by accusing the president's brother of involvement in a railroad swindle. Eager to restore his reputation as a brave, dashing leader, Custer split his force in two and also decided not to wait for a larger army force to catch up with his column.

The Sioux and Cheyenne war parties were led by Sitting Bull, who was reluctant to fight a pitched battle against a large cavalry force. Younger chiefs, however, including Gall and Low Dog, spoke passionately for war and the other warrior leaders eagerly agreed.

The summer of 1876 was the time of a great celebration, especially in Philadelphia, where Americans were marking the nation's centennial—one hundred years since declaring independence from Great Britain. While people marveled at the many modern exhibits, they were also fascinated by news from the frontier, especially the Indian Wars. While anticipating news of great deeds by the dashing General Custer and his troopers, they were stunned instead by news of the expedition's fate as shown in the following selections. The battle took place on June 25, but news did not reach the East until July 5.

FROM

The New York Times

JULY 6, 1876

GEN CUSTER AND SEVENTEEN COMMISSIONED OFFICERS
BUTCHERED IN A BATTLE OF THE LITTLE HORN —ATTACK
ON AN OVERWHELMINGLY LARGE CAMP OF SAVAGES—
THREE HUNDRED AND FIFTEEN MEN KILLED—THE
BATTLEFIELD LIKE A SLAUGHTER PEN

A Fuller Report From the Scene as General Terry Arrives.

They met a sight to apall the stoutest heart . . . General Custer had evidently attempted to attack the village . . . which was about two miles long and a mile wide. At the highest point of the ridge they found Custer, surrounded by his chosen band. Here were his two brothers and his nephew, all lying within a circle of a few yards, their horses beside them. Here the last stand had been made, and here one after another of this last survivors of Custer's five companies had met their death. . . . Not a man had escaped to tell the tale, but it was inscribed on these barren hills in a language more elegant than words.

. . . It is obvious that the troops were completely surrounded by a force ten times their number. . . . Information from Army sources leads to the conclusion that 2,500 or 3,000 Indians composed the fighting force arrayed against Custer and his 600.

A Death Sonnet for Custer

On July 10, 1876, four days after news of the battle at Little Bighorn reached the East, poet Walt Whitman published the following poem in the *New York Tribune*.

> . . . Thou of the sunny, flowing hair, in battle,
> I erewhile now, with erect head, pressing
>   ever in front, bearing a bright sword
>   in thy hand,
> Now ending well the splendid favor of thy
>   deeds, (I bring no dirge for it or thee—
>   I bring a glad, triumphal sonnet;)
> There in the far northwest, in struggle,
>   charge, and saber-smite,
> Desperate and glorious—aye in defeat
>   most desperate, most glorious,
> After thy many battles, in which, never
>   yielding up a gun or a color,
> Leaving behind thee a memory sweet to
>   soldiers
> Thou yieldest up thyself.
>
> —Walt Whitman, 1876

ֆֆ ֆֆ ֆֆ ֆֆ ֆֆ ֆֆ ֆֆ ֆֆ ֆֆ ֆֆ ֆֆ ֆֆ ֆֆ ֆֆ ֆֆ

FROM
Chief Low Dog's Account
1 8 8 1

They came on us like a thunderbolt. I never before nor since saw men so brave and fearless as those white warriors. We retreated until our men got all together, and then we charged upon them. I called to my men, "This is a good day to die: follow me!" We massed our men, and that no man should fall back, every man whipped another man's horse and we rushed right upon them. . . . The white warriors dismounted to fire. . . . They held their horses reins on one arm while they were shooting, but their horses were so frightened that they pulled the men all around, and a great many of their shots went up in the air. . . . I did not see Gen. Custer. . . . We did not know . . . that he was the white chief.

"Blacks in Blue"

In the years following the Civil War, a war-weary nation had little interest in paying for a large army cavalry to fight the Native American tribes of the West. By 1866 the army had only 54,000 men and that number was soon cut in half. One solution was to recruit African Americans who were eager for work of any kind. Blacks had fought well in the Civil War and many white army officers supported the idea of having them in the cavalry. But other officers objected and the issue caused considerable debate in Congress. Once the idea was approved, the African American troopers found themselves stationed in the least desirable frontier forts, where they usually received substandard supplies. The blacks, who were called "blacks in blue" (referring to the blue uniforms) by news reporters and "buffalo soldiers" by the Native Americans, proved to be outstanding soldiers and made up 20 percent of the soldiers in the West. The Ninth and Tenth Cavalry Regiments were particularly effective in fighting the rugged

Apache warriors in the desert Southwest. Eleven of the men were awarded the Congressional Medal of Honor. The following selection is from the debate in the Senate in 1866. Henry Wilson, a Republican from Massachusetts, responded to the negative voices with the following statement.

FROM

Senator Henry Wilson's Speech

1 8 6 6

Our cavalry regiments will be mostly our frontier regiments; and while we have desertions, and have had lately since the war has been over, to the extent of thirty or forty percent, from our white regiments that go on the frontiers, there are no desertions from the colored regiments stationed in Arkansas and on the frontiers, and they are the best riders in America connected with our Army. . . . I think it is a matter of great economy to put some of these colored regiments into the field in the Indian country, in the mountains, and in sections of the country where white men desert largely and go to the mines where the temptation is very great.

LIBRARY OF CONGRESS

Buffalo soldiers, 1890.

Chief Joseph and the Flight of the Nez Perce

After the Battle of the Little Bighorn, the Indian Wars became a matter of the army forcing tribe after tribe to give up and move on to reservations. Americans welcomed the news reports of each army victory; most had come to feel that the Indians deserved punishment.

A strange twist occurred in the autumn of 1877, when a small tribe of Nez Perce rebelled against an army order opening part of their reservation on the Idaho-Oregon border to settlement. Led by Chief Joseph, they went into hiding in White Bird Canyon, but they were forced to fight to drive back an army unit. Chief Joseph decided to try to lead his people to safety in Canada. With only about 150 warriors and 550 women, children, and older men, Chief Joseph led the way through the Bitteroot Mountains toward Canada. General Oliver O. Howard was in pursuit with several army detachments.

At first the public cheered as the army seemed close to crushing the tribe. But then public opinion did a complete flip-flop, as sympathy for the Indians increased. People's hearts went out to this ragged, courageous band as they struggled through the barren cold of Montana Territory. Several times, Joseph's warriors turned and fought to gain a little more time. When Howard's troopers finally surrounded the half-starved band and forced their surrender, they were less than thirty miles from the Canadian border. The heroic flight had covered seventeen hundred miles and lasted three months.

The following selection is Chief Joseph's statement to General Howard. His words became famous as a summary of the tragedy that had befallen the Indians of the Great Plains.

FROM

Chief Joseph's Statement

OCTOBER 1871

Tell General Howard I know his heart. What he told me before I have in my heart. I am tired of fighting. Our chiefs are killed. Looking Glass is dead. Too-hul-hul-sote is dead. The old men are all dead. It is the young men who say yes or no. He who led on the young men is dead. It is cold and we have no blankets. The little children are freezing to death. My people, some of them, have run away to the hills, and have no blankets, no food; no one knows where they are—perhaps freezing to death. I want to have time to look for my children and see how many of them I can find. Maybe I shall find them among the dead. Hear me, my chiefs. I am tired; my heart is sick and sad. From where the sun now stands I will fight no more forever.

Ho for Kansas!

Brethren, Friends, & Fellow Citizens:
I feel thankful to inform you that the

REAL ESTATE
AND
Homestead Association,
Will Leave Here the

15th of April, 1878,

In pursuit of Homes in the Southwestern Lands of America, at Transportation Rates, cheaper than ever was known before.

For full information inquire of
Benj. Singleton, better known as old Pap,
NO. 5 NORTH FRONT STREET.
Beware of Speculators and Adventurers, as it is a dangerous thing to fall in their hands.

Nashville, Tenn., March 18, 1878.

One of the many posters calling on southern blacks to leave for Kansas.

Posters like this encouraged African Americans to settle in Kansas. With the help of churches, African Americans formed homestead associations and headed west. In 1878, more than six thousand black Americans joined this migration.

The Last Land Rush

At the time of the Indian Removal Policy in the 1800s, the Indian tribes were granted a huge land area west of the Mississippi River. As white settlers pushed relentlessly westward, however, the "Indian Territory" was repeatedly shrunken until it included little more than present-day Oklahoma.

In 1889, a large part of Oklahoma, purchased from the tribes, was going to be opened to settlement. By this time there was no other unclaimed land anywhere in the country, so thousands of people were eager to have a piece of it. The government announced that the land could be claimed starting at noon on April 22, 1889. Settlers, known as "Boomers," could not start until the signal was given; Army patrols held everyone back. Hamilton S. Wick describes his experience as a Boomer. Nearly one hundred thousand others joined in the scramble.

FROM

Hamilton Wick's Report

1889

Many of the "boomers" were mounted on high-spirited and fleet-footed horses, and had ranged themselves along the territorial line, scarcely restrained even by the presence of the troop of cavalry. . . . The . . . wagons and carriages ranged themselves in line with the horsemen, and even here and there mule teams attached to canvas-covered vehicles stood in the front ranks. . . . All was excitement and expectation. . . . Suddenly the air was pierced with the blast of a bugle. Hundreds of throats echoed the sound with shouts of exultation. The quivering limbs of saddled steeds, no longer restrained by the hands that held their bridles, bounded forward simultaneously into the "beautiful land" of Oklahoma; and wagons and carriages and buggies and prairie schooners . . . joined in this . . . race. . . .

All that there was of Guthrie . . . on April 22, at 1:30 P.M., when the first train from the north drew up at the station . . . was a water-tank, a small station-house, a shanty for the Wells, Fargo Express, and a Government Land Office. . . .

I remember throwing my blankets out of the car window the instant the train stopped at the station. I remember tumbling after them through the self-same window. Then I joined the wild scramble for a town lot. . . . I found myself . . . about midway between the government building and depot. It occurred to me that a street would probably run past the depot. I [hailed] a man who looked like a deputy, and asked him if this was to be a street. . . .

"Yes," he replied. "We are laying off four corner lots right here for a lumber yard."

"Is this the corner where I stand?" I inquired.

"Yes," he responded, approaching me.

"Boomers" and "Sooners"

The people who took part in the last land rush, or land boom, were called "Boomers." There were also hundreds of "Sooners"— people who tried to sneak in ahead of the signal to start. While many Sooners lost their claims, they gave a nickname to Oklahoma as the "Sooner State."

"Then I claim this corner lot!" I said with decision, as I jammed my location stick in the ground and hammered it . . . home with my heel.

I proceeded at once to unstrap a small folding cot I brought with me, and by standing it on its end it made a tolerable center-pole for a tent. I then threw a couple of my blankets over the cot, and staked them securely into the ground on either side. Thus I had a claim that was unjumpable because of substantial improvements. . . . As night approached I strolled up [to] the land office, and surveyed the . . . [scene] spread out before me. . . . Ten thousand people had "squatted" upon a square mile of virgin prairie that first afternoon.

Staking a claim to land in Oklahoma Territory in the last great land rush, 1889.

SOURCES

PART I: Crossing the First Mountain Barrier

John Filson, *The Adventures of Colonel Daniel Boone*, 1784: reprinted in Robert W. Richmond and Robert W. Mardock, eds., *A Nation Moving West: Readings in the History of the American Frontier* (Lincoln: University of Nebraska Press, 1966), pp. 9f.

Colonel John May's Journal, 1788: from *Colonel John May, Journal and Letters . . . Relative to Two Journeys to the Ohio Country in 1788 and 1789* (Cincinnati: Ohio Historical Society, 1873); reprinted in Albert Bushnell Hart, ed., *American History as Told by Contemporaries*, vol. 1 (New York: Macmillan Co., 1897, 1925), p. 261.

PART II: Jefferson and the West

John Boit, *Voyages of the "Columbia" to the Northwest Coast, 1787–1790 and 1790–1793*, 1792: from the edition edited by Frederick William Howay (Boston: Massachusetts Historical Society, 1941), pp. 216f.

Journals of Lewis and Clark, 1805: from Reuben Gold Thwaites, ed., *Original Journals of the Lewis and Clark Expedition* (New York: Dodd, Mead & Co., 1904, 1905), pp. 112f.

Journal of Merriwether Lewis, 1805: adapted from Paul M. Angle, ed., *The American Reader: From Columbus to Today* (Boston and Chicago: Rand McNally & Co., 1958), pp. 161–162.

PART III: Transportation in the Old Northwest

Charles Latrobe, *The Rambler in North America*, c. 1825: 2 vols. (London: R.B.Seeley & W. Burnside, 1835), reprinted in Richmond and Mardock, *A Nation Moving West*, pp. 83f.

Frederick Gerstaecker's Journal, c. 1832: from Frederick Gerstaecker, *Wild Sports in the Old West* (Boston, 1859), reprinted in *ibid.*, pp. 93–94.

John Hall's Letters, 1827: from John Hall, *Letters from the West* (London, 1828), reprinted in Angle, *The American Reader*, pp. 124f.

H. S. Tanner, *Emigrant's and Traveller's Guide to the West*, 1834: from the facsimile edition (Pennsylvania Historical Society, 1976).

Timothy Flint, *Recollections of the Last Ten Years*, 1826: reprinted in American Heritage, *History of the Growth of the United States* (New York: American Heritage Publishing Co., 1968), p. 167.

PART IV: Daily Life in the Old Northwest

Timothy Flint, *Recollections of the Last Ten Years*, 1826: reprinted in Charles G. Sellers, ed., *As It Happened: A History of the United States* (New York: McGraw-Hill, 1975), p. 174.

Edward W. Barber, "Recollections and Lessons of Pioneer Boyhood," c. 1840: from Michigan Pioneer and Historical Society Collection, XXXI, 1902, reprinted in Richmond and Mardock, *A Nation Moving West*, pp. 106–107.

Peter Cartwright's Autobiography, 1856: from W. P. Strickland, *The Autobiography of Peter Cartwright, the Backwoods Preacher* (Cincinnati and New York: Hunt & Eaton, 1856); reprinted in Hart, *American History as Told by Contemporaries*, vol. 1, p. 311.

Samuel Brown's Report, 1817: adapted from *The Western Gazeteer or the Emigrant's Directory* (Auburn, N.Y.: H. C. Southwick, 1817; reprint, New York State Historical Association, 1947), pp. 22f.

PART V: Native American Resistance and the Indian Removal Policy

General Sam Dale's Report on Tecumseh, 1811: adapted from Carl F. Klinck, *Tecumseh: Fact and Fiction in Early Records* (Englewood Cliffs, N.J.: Prentice-Hall, 1961), pp. 131f.

President Jackson's Letter to Congress, 1832: from Jame D. Richardson, ed., *A Compilation of the Messages & Papers of the Presidents* (New York: Bureau of National Literature, 1897; reprint, Northern Illinois University, 2002), p. 1128.

Anonymous Eyewitness Account, 1839: from the *New York Observer*, January 26, 1839; reprinted in John Ehle, *Trail of Tears: The Rise and Fall of the Cherokee Nation* (New York: Doubleday, 1988), pp. 112f.

Major Elliott's Journal, 1834: adapted from Margaret Coit and the editors of LIFE, *Life History of the United States*, vol. 4, *The Sweep Westward* (Alexandria, Va.: Time-Life, 1963), p. 43.

Part VI: The Southern Frontier

Olmstead's Travel Journal, c. 1835: from Frederick Law
Olmstead, *A Journey in the Back Country* (New York:
1863), pp. 129–130; reprinted in Norman R. Yetman,
ed., *Life Under the Peculiar Institution* (New York: Holt,
Rinehart & Winston, 1965), p. 234.

Colonel Travis's Appeal for Help, 1836: adapted and
abridged from Angle, *The American Reader,* pp.
235–236.

Stephen Austin's statements quoted in Edward S. Barnard,
ed., *Story of the Great American West* (Pleasantville, N.Y.:
Reader's Digest Corp., 1977), p. 125.

Davy Crockett's Journal, 1836: from Davy Crockett, *The
Life of Davy Crockett* (New York: A.L. Burt Co., 1902);
reprinted in David Colbert, ed., *Eyewitness to the
American West* (New York: Penguin Group, 1998),
pp. 95f.

Sam Houston's Report, 1836: adapted from "Official
Report of General Sam Houston on the Battle of San
Jacinto," in Henderson Youkum, *History of Texas;*
reprinted in David C. King et al., *United States History:
Readings* (Menlo Park, Cal.: Addison-Wesley Co.,
1988), pp. 46–47.

PART VII: Opening the Far West

Reverend Samuel Parker's Journal, 1835: from Samuel
Parker, *Journal of an Exploring Tour Beyond the Rocky
Mountains* (Ithaca, N.Y., 1842); reprinted in Richmond
and Mardock, *A Nation Moving West,* pp. 120f.

James Beckwourth's Recollections, c. 1855: adapted from
The Life and Adventures of James P. Beckwourth,
written from his own dictation by T. D. Bonner (New
York: Harper & Brothers, 1856); reprinted in Hart,
American History as Told by Contemporaries, vol. 2,
pp. 88f.

Narcissa Whitman's Diary, 1836: adapted from T. C. Elliot,
comp., *The Coming of the White Women, 1836, as Told in
Letters and Journals of Narcissa Prentiss Whitman*
(Portland: Oregon Historical Society, 1937); facsimile
edition (Bedford, Mass.: Applewood Books, 1987),
pp. 46f.

PART VIII: Wagons West! Life on the Trails

Jesse Applegate's Account, 1846: from Jesse Applegate, "A
Day with the Cow Column in 1843," in *Recollections of
My Boyhood* (Rosebud, Ore.: Review Publishing Co.,
1914), pp. 243f.

Amelia Knight's Diary, 1853: from Amelia Stewart Knight,
Diary (Transactions of the 56th Annual Reunion of the
Oregon Pioneer Association, 1928); reprinted in Josef
Berger and Dorothy Berger, *Diary of America* (New
York: Simon & Schuster, 1957), pp. 340–349.

Betsey Bayley's Letter, 1849: adapted from Holmes, in
ibid., p. 37.

Stephen and Mariah King's Letter, 1846: from *ibid,* pp.
44–45.

Harriet Ward's Diary, 1853: from Harriet Sherrill Ward,
Prairie Schooner Lady, 1853; from the edition edited by
Ward D. Dewitt and Florence Stark Dewitt (Los Ange-
les: Western Lore Press, 1959), pp. 66–67.

Esther Hanna's Diary, 1855: adapted from John Mark
Faragher, *Women and Men on the Overland Trail* (New
Haven: Yale University Press, 2001), p. 179.

Virginia E. B. Reed's Letter, 1847: adapted from George R.
Stewart, *Ordeal by Hunger* (Boston: Houghton Mifflin,
1960), pp. 355–362.

William Clayton's Journal, 1847: from William Muller and
A. Russell Mortensen, eds., *Among the Mormons: His-
toric Accounts by Contemporary Observers* (Lincoln:
University of Nebraska Press, 1973), p. 183.

Brigham Young's Discourse, 1847: from *ibid.,* p. 246.

PART IX: The Gold Rush and the Mining Frontier

James W. Marshall's Account, 1848: from Charles B. Gille-
spie, "Marshall's Own Account of the Gold Discovery,"
Century Magazine, February 1891; reprinted in Emily
Davie, comp., *Profile of America* (New York: Thomas Y.
Crowell, 1954), p. 151.

John Hawkins Clark's Journal, 1852: from "Overland to
the Gold Fields," Richmond and Mardock, *A Nation
Moving West,* pp. 169f.

"Shirley Letters," 1851: from Louisa Amelia Knapp Smith
Clappe, *The Shirley Letters from the California Mines*
(New York: Knopf, 1949), pp. 22f.

Old Block's Pen-Knife Sketches, 1853: from Alonzo Delano
aka "Old Block," *Pen-Knife Sketches* (Sacramento,
1853); reprinted in Davidson, *Life in America,* vol. 1,
pp. 256f.

St. Joseph Newspaper Account, 1865: from *St. Joseph Weekly
West,* April 17, 1865; reprinted in Davidson, *Life in
America,* vol. 2, pp. 262–263.

Mark Twain, *Roughing It,* 1872: from Davidson, *ibid.,*
p. 274.

PART X: From Sea to Shining Sea

Recollections of Thomas Nichols, c. 1840: from Thomas
Low Nichols, *Forty Years of American Life* (London,
1864); reprinted in Sellers, *As It Happened,* p. 162.

William Richardson's Diary, 1846: from William H. Richardson, *A Private Soldier in the Campaign of New and Old Mexico, Under the Command of Colonel Doniphan* (Baltimore, 1849); reprinted in Davie, *Profile of America*, 229f.

Frederick Douglass's *The North Star*, 1848: from *Story of the Great American West* (Pleasantville, N.Y.: Reader's Digest Association, 1977), p. 174.

The Homestead Act, 1862: from www.pbs.org/weta/ thewest/resources/archives/five/homestd.htm.

PART XI: Railroads and Cattle Drives

Alta California, 1868: from the *Story of the Great American West*, p. 257.

New York Daily Tribune, 1868: from *ibid*.

New York Daily Tribune, Front Page, May 11, 1869: from Davidson, *Life in America*, vol. 2, p. 268.

Bret Harte's Tribute, 1869: from King, *United States History*, p. 311.

New York Times, 1870: from Davidson, *Life in America*, vol. 2, pp. 276–277.

Cowhand Jim McCawley's Account, 1887: from James Emmit McCauley, *A Stove-up Cowboy's Story* (Dallas: Texas Folklore Association; Southern Methodist University Press, 1943), pp. 5–6.

Andy Adams's Account, 1866: from Davidson, *Life in America*, vol. 1, p. 432.

Theodore Roosevelt's Autobiography, 1885: from *ibid.*, p. 436.

John W. Clampitt's Account, 1889: from John Clampitt, *Echoes from the Rocky Mountains* (Chicago: Belford, Clarke & Co., 1889), pp. 494f.

John W. Clampitt's Account, 1889: from *ibid*.

Theodore Roosevelt's Autobiography, 1885: from Davidson, *Life in America*, vol. 1, p. 443.

New York Sun, 1888: from Sellers, *As It Happened*, p. 224.

PART XII: The Last Indian Wars and the Closing of the Frontier

Charles Reed's Description, c. 1868: from Charles Reed, "Life in a Nebraska Soddy," *Nebraska History 39* (March 1958), p. 59; reprinted in Richmond and Mardock, *A Nation Moving West*, pp. 306f.

George Catlin's Account, c. 1836: from George Catlin, *North American Indians, Being Notes on Their Life and Conditions* (London, 1843); reprinted in Berger, *Diary of America*, p. 274.

Captain Alexander Stewart's Letter, 1844: adapted from Hart, *American History as Told by Contemporaries*, vol. 2, p. 226.

George Ramspert's Account, 1881: from George W. Ramspert, *The Western Echo* (Dayton United Brethren Publishing Co., 1881); reprinted in Martin Ridge, *Liberty and Union* (Boston: Houghton Mifflin, 1972), vol. 2, p. 102.

William Webb's Account, 1872: from William Webb, *Buffalo Land* (Cincinnati & Chicago: E. Hannaford & Co., 1872; reprint, New York State Historical Assoc., 1969), pp. 312–314.

New York Times, July 6, 1876: adapted from Lally Weymouth, *America in 1876* (New York: Random House, 1976), pp. 60f.

Chief Low Dog's Account, 1881: from the *Leavenworth Weekly Times*, August 18, 1881; reprinted in *The Story of the Great American West*, p. 234.

Walt Whitman, "A Death Sonnet for Custer," 1876: from the *New York Tribune*, July 10, 1876; reprinted in Weymouth, *America in 1876*, p. 267.

Senator Henry Wilson's Speech, 1866: from Colbert, *Eyewitness to the American West*, p. 157.

Chief Joseph's Statement, 1871: from King et al., *United States History*, p. 343.

Hamilton Wick's Report, 1889: adapted from Ridge, *Liberty & Union*, vol. 2, p. 188.

INDEX